G000108887

My Pilgrim Way

Other books by Gerald Priestland

America: The Changing Nation
Frying Tonight: The Saga of Fish and Chips
The Future of Violence
The Dilemmas of Journalism
Yours Faithfully
West of Hayle River *(with photographs by Sylvia Priestland)*
Yours Faithfully volume 2
Priestland's Progress
Who Needs the Church?
Priestland Right and Wrong
Gerald Priestland at Large
The Case Against God
Something Understood: An Autobiography
The Unquiet Suitcase
Priestlands' Cornwall (with Sylvia Priestland)

My Pilgrim Way

LATE WRITINGS

Gerald Priestland

Edited by Roger Toulmin

MOWBRAY

Mowbray
A Cassell imprint
Villiers House, 41/47 Strand, London WC2N 5JE
387 Park Avenue South, New York, NY 10016–8810

© Sylvia Priestland 1993

All rights reserved. No part of this publication may be reproduced or transmitted in any form or by any means, electronic or mechanical including photocopying, recording or any information storage or retrieval system, without prior permission in writing from the publishers.

First published 1993

British Library Cataloguing-in-Publication Data
A catalogue record for this book is available from the British Library

Library of Congress Cataloging-in-Publication Data applied for.

ISBN 0–264–67310–7

Cover photograph by kind permission of Sylvia Priestland

Typeset by Colset Pte Ltd, Singapore
Printed and bound in Great Britain by
Biddles Ltd, Guildford and King's Lynn

Contents

Acknowledgements

I am delighted that Rosemary Hartill, former Religious Affairs Correspondent at the BBC following my husband, becoming a friend who knew him so well, has written this foreword.

Also, I wish particularly to thank Roger Toulmin who edited this book, and despite his own serious illness, spent much valuable time making this selection of the material left by my husband.

Sylvia Priestland
London, February 1993

Memoir of Gerald Priestland

Rosemary Hartill

When T. S. Eliot was awarded the Nobel Prize in 1948, he was asked by a reporter why he thought he had been so honoured. Eliot, unwilling to pick out any particular poem or play, replied that he assumed it was for the entire corpus. 'Oh yes', said the reporter, taking a careful note. 'And when did you publish that?'

This collection of talks by Gerald Priestland is the completion of Gerry's 'corpus'. Over thirty years as a BBC news correspondent, he broadcast to a mass audience thousands and thousands of scripts; he published lively reflections on America, on fish and chips, on violence, on Cornwall. A book on the media reflected on the ethical dilemmas implicit in his trade. After becoming the BBC's religious affairs correspondent in 1977, he wrote several books on God; and on retirement looked back on his life in an autobiography *Something Understood* (1986). These talks cover the last ten years of his life.

On 22 June 1989, he suffered a stroke. The effect was devastating. After four months in hospital and some twenty months at home, he was able once again to dress himself (it took an hour), and get around very slowly. His right leg 'hurt like hell', and his right arm was almost useless. The final talks, pecked out laboriously on the typewriter with one finger of his left hand, reflect on these sufferings, his last spiritual voyage. The last one, unfinished, was in his typewriter at his death.

Gerry Priestland was never a press-ganged voyager. From the beginning of his highly successful broadcasting career, he was an enthusiastic midshipman, then senior officer, on the BBC's various tramp ships around the world. Following orders, he was regularly put ashore at some port of call, and from there would relay reports back to Britain of what was happening, what it was like to be there.

This collection tells some of the story of what happened

when, after thirty years of naval service, he was finally allowed to retire. Here is a man now free to sail his own private yacht to wherever he has a whim to visit. Signals from various ports flash in, inviting him to reflect on his travels. Churches want sermons, universities request lectures or seminars, marriage guidance councils seek new perspectives. Some of the topics he chose himself; others were chosen for him. There are reflections on Church unity, on the Church of the future, on vice and virtue, on the saints; but whatever the subject, the underlying question he keeps returning to is 'How should we best lead our lives?'

But gradually, not just the winds, but another undercurrent is pulling, one which gradually grows into a tide no one can resist. He recognizes some of the navigational features of the new landscape, but is unsure about others. He describes them more and more, and starts to reflect on the undiscovered country to which he now knows he is being drawn. Before he reaches it, like St Paul, he undergoes shipwreck, and finally salvage.

I first met Gerry Priestland rather late in his career. It was about 1977, shortly after he had become the BBC's religious affairs correspondent. The 'corpus' that immediately struck you was his body. At 6 foot 6, he had a towering physical presence, led at the front by a strapping beer belly. The delight of the religious affairs department in having him was matched only by its collective awe of his person. As a lone news correspondent, and anchorman, he was hugely experienced, and hugely professional; moreover, though generally very nice and modest to everyone, he was also known to be capable of occasional bouts of sudden fury, and did not suffer fools or incompetents gladly.

Religious broadcasting was then sited in offices on the second floor of Broadcasting House, overlooking Portland Place. Gerry shared his smallish office with his part-time secretary Pam Almaz. She was hardly at all in awe of him, and treated him rather like a delightful schoolboy. Gerry would proudly boast to his old newsroom drinking pals that at night she danced in the West End show *The Best Little Whore-House in Texas*. A squawk box in the corner would relay newsflashes from the newsroom.

In a corner of Gerry's office, at the bottom of a large steel cabinet, was the Priestland Collection of Plugs and Cables for All Occasions. Into the mysteries of these technical rituals Gerry initiated me when, in 1979, I was recruited as his assistant, with the title of BBC religious affairs reporter. Gerry had been taken ill in Mexico during a papal visit, and had subsequently been promised an assistant by Colin Semper, then head of department, to release him from the news treadmill. My job was to take over as much as possible of the day-to-day religious news reporting. This freed him to make *Priestland's Progress* and other series for Radio 4, in which his aim was to make basic Christian doctrines accessible, in a lively and entertaining way, to those outside the Church. Those belonging to 'the church of the unchurched' were always his favourite audience in those years.

When he first joined the BBC newsroom in 1949, the atmosphere surrounding the news bulletins was, as he put it, 'a compound of holiness, patriotism and the Gold Standard . . . a pompous and soporific news service'. 'Remember, Priestland', he was told by one news editor, as he was struggling over some particularly deadly and boring item about national savings, 'there's no harm in being dull.' That appalled him, and it always appalled him. Gerry was a superb entertainer, as well as a superb journalist.

Working his way up from obituarist and conveyor of weather forecasts, he applied for the job of correspondent in India. His autobiography claims nobody went to India willingly – it was a notorious hardship post and communications were so bad that the correspondent hardly ever got on the air. But the romance of the place attracted him, and at 26 he was appointed as foreign correspondent for India, Pakistan, Burma and Ceylon – the youngest BBC correspondent ever appointed. He was sent out on probation for six months, his wife, Sylvia, abandoned on the orders of BBC newsroom higher command, to bear the second of their four children at home without him. His job was, as he put it, 'to attempt the magic trick of persuading listeners thousands of miles away what it was like'. His great skill was not so much in interviewing, as in spotting interesting news stories, painting word pictures and stories, combining vivid colour, wit and pace with shrewd analysis.

Later he moved to America, to the Middle East and other key posts. He reported on the civil rights campaigns in America, and the Vietnam war. Then he did some TV newscasting, and fronted the technically disastrous opening of BBC2, when he had to ad lib for what felt like an eternity.

Then he presented an evening radio programme called *Newsdesk* where, reporting 'news with a human voice', he found himself in the business of near-editorializing. He amused himself by seeing how close to the wind he could get. He said he was not interested in pushing any particular political line, but in exposing folly and pomposity, sometimes evoking pity, even confessing hilarity or boredom. It was a path he followed later, to the irritation of some.

One news-gathering trip took him back to Saigon. He found it as deeply addicted as ever to violence, and ended up weeping in a hotel room. He wrote his wife a letter of such desolation that she was left as devastated as he was. In his autobiography, he wrote 'I knew I had committed a crime, the penalty for which was death, but precisely what it was I could not say. Probably it had to do with the utter fraudulence of my success.' After many sessions on the couch of a Viennese analyst, he joined the Society of Friends.

By now, he did not want to go abroad again – it was too dangerous, and he felt he could not stand the pace any more. He thought he would like to become religious affairs correspondent. It would give him opportunities to travel and to 'poke my nose into almost any subject that took my fancy'. If there was any sense to be made of the pleasures and horrors he had experienced in the past twenty-seven years, this was where to attempt it. When the appointment was announced in 1977, 'half of my friends backed away as if I had confessed to a sex-change operation, the other half started telling me things they had always wanted to tell somebody'.

He held the post for five years. To begin with, he shared an office with Monica Furlong and Ron Farrow. They laughed so much that in the end he thought it best that they separated, so that they could get on with more work. His first summer was spent recording a tragi-comic montage of the woes of parish organists in a programme called *Seated One Day*.

He soon branched out further. 'The fact was', he wrote, 'that there was a very limited number of religious stories I could persuade the cynical news department to run, and if I had not branched out as a self-made guru, there would not have been much satisfaction in the job.' As a foreign correspondent, he had been lucky to get half-a-dozen letters a year; now he began to get half-a-dozen a day, partly due to his Saturday morning talks *Yours Faithfully*, and the prize-winning *Priestland's Progress*. In a Radio 4 poll for 'Man of the Year' he got more votes than the Pope.

A journalist is usually at his or her best when she or he has just discovered something fascinating, and wants to share it with someone else. That happened when he became religious affairs correspondent. It was as if his Viennese analyst released a spiritual dam. In his autobiography, he managed to describe most of his life up to his breakdown with hardly any reference to a spiritual journey. This collection of essays helps explain why.

For years, he suppressed feelings of anger, and violence and despair, and Christianity seemed to be an aggravator of this despair. Every crucified Christ, he tells us, reproached him: 'You did this to me.' When at last, after his analysis, he came to trust himself to love himself, to feel able to forgive himself, then his spiritual life was released. And he was able to speak of his religious experience with a freshness, mixed with a trenchant commonsense, that made his words accessible to people who had a healthy resistance to religious jargon and cliché.

Gerry rarely gave himself an easy time. Instead he *used* his horrors and pleasures to build bridges for other people, to make them feel less alone, less isolated. And how he made all of us laugh.

So, how do these last talks differ from those he wrote when still working full time for the BBC? There are still examples of his bravura showpiece style as in 'Vices and Virtues'. But let loose from the tight corset of broadcasting, for a while his stylistic girth expands, becomes at times a shade more corpulent. Occasionally, he is tempted into the waterways of self-assertion, rather than description. But then this retired sailor, pretending to potter about the waterways, uttering the occasional deliberate naval heresy to provoke the officers, will suddenly focus our minds:

> Doctrine, I think, is a tool to work with, a rope to help us climb the mountain – not an image to be worshipped for itself.
>
> There is no such thing as an abstract moral question – there are only particular moral cases.
>
> Under God, nobody has rights; only duties.
>
> [The Home Secretary told us that] the Church was uniquely placed to provide the nation with moral

> leadership. 'That authority', he declared, 'rests firmly with the Church.' Alas, the Church today is very *badly* placed, and its authority is most *in*firm.

Finally, the swelling tide concentrated his mind wonderfully. In these last talks, he wrestles again and again with the key questions of life and death. How should we lead our lives? What will happen after death? What does resurrection mean? How will we be judged? Is there a loophole?

For me, the most beautiful talk is 'At a stroke', broadcast on the World Service, written painfully and slowly after the shipwreck of a stroke that initially had left him babbling complete nonsense. I cannot read it without tears, for here he charts how the simple action of a young nurse once more showed him that true love is given regardless of merit. It was the beginning of his redemption.

I saw him at home in Golders Green that winter of 1990/91. It was one of those magical days of winter light reflecting from deep snow. He was able only to shuffle around, his right side mostly paralysed, and his foot feeling as if trapped in a mincing machine. But he could type with one finger, could converse cheerfully, and could get out once a week to wine-tasting sessions – now a restricted pleasure for the new slimmed-down Priestland. He had just discovered a new Indian champagne called Omar Khayyam. Despite all the terrible wrestling, wounded like Jacob in the Bible story, God had blessed him and his artist wife Sylvia. He was more benign, more mellow, more peaceful, than I had ever known him. That day will stand in my memory years on from now.

I know he is now held in the hand of God, and I am happy for him.

Introductory

1
On My Pilgrim Way

'Too much Priestland, not enough progress'
(review in *The Universe*)

I have had as many churches in my time as a rather flashy film star has had wives – though I have never regarded myself as divorced from any of them, so perhaps I am a religious polygamist. Yet I am not ashamed of it. It is not my purpose to advocate plural membership for everyone; but if you do some day feel the urge to move on as I did, my advice is not to feel ashamed, and not to feel that you must let go of everything in your past – for in the life of the spirit, no experience need ever be wasted.

I was brought up a public-school Anglican – chapel every morning and twice on Sundays, House prayers every evening and a Scripture lesson every day. As a classics scholar I had to do the New Testament in Greek – a mean way of getting in yet another Greek lesson.

I took most of my theology not from the Book of Common Prayer (which was largely unintelligible) but from the *English Hymnal*, particularly those numbers in it that dripped with sin and blood. I came away from my prep school with a pretty melancholy impression of the Christian faith, which taught me that not only had I done those things I ought not to have done and left undone an intolerable number of things I ought to have done, but that despite my most conscientious efforts – for I was a nauseatingly *good* boy – *there was no health in me.*

I went on to one of our great – equally Anglican – public schools where the hymn-book was slightly more optimistic but the Prayer Book was still the order of service and becoming oppressively intelligible. It seemed to me that what was going on was the vainest of repetition and an insult to human nature. If

God had made us, how could there be 'no health in us'? And there was all this business of Christ dying for our sins. How could he? They were our sins, not his, and if in spite of his dying we continued to sin as wickedly as ever – *and* had to take the responsibility for it – what was the point? It was very unfair on Jesus; and as for being invited to eat his flesh and drink his blood – it was barbarous and disgusting. Anyway, by that time I had read Fraser's *Golden Bough* and knew all about sacrificial kings.

So I became the school atheist and refused to bob my head during the Creed. Everyone else was rather shocked; not because they were particularly devout (the only really devout boy in the school was William Rees-Mogg, but then Catholics did not count), but because it simply was not done. The school chapel commemorated hundreds of Old Boys killed in the two World Wars, and we sang 'I vow to thee, my country' till the windows shook. So there was an odour of unpatriotism about my atheism.

Which lasted until I was about eighteen and won a scholarship to Oxford. My induction involved taking a long Latin oath, at the end of which the Warden of the college shook me by the hand, told me I was now an *ex officio* deacon of the Church of England and would have to wear a frock in chapel. Since the college choir was extremely good and sang beautiful Tudor services every evening, I wanted to go to chapel very much. You might say I underwent a forcible conversion. But it was not that simple.

For a start, it was cold outside, trying to be coolly rational in a culture which still expressed so many of its deepest feelings in Christian terms. It so happened that at Oxford the school of logical positivism – which maintained that no statement had any meaning unless it corresponded with some measurable experience – still held sway over philosophy. Logically it followed that theological and religious statements were meaningless. I am still grateful to my philosophy tutors for teaching me to be careful in the use of language – to ask myself all the time 'Does that really *mean* anything?' But useful though it was, far from destroying religion for me, positivism only convinced me that here was something of a different order of seriousness: because what religion said to me – and for me – corresponded to experiences that were more real and personal than most of those handled by philosophy. The positivist school may sharpen the mind, but it is sterile, and in the end destroys itself; one can only end up doubting whether philosophy itself has any meaning, whether it is even possible. Religion, on the other hand, seems endlessly creative. It goes on and on, constantly referring to the experiences of life and being confirmed by them. In short, I found religion much more interesting than theory of knowledge, and to the distress of the logical people I took moral philosophy, which they regard as a disreputable pursuit.

But just as important as all this, I met my wife at Oxford, and all her family were English Presbyterians. So off I went to St Columba's and was confirmed in what is now the United Reformed Church. I liked the four-square Scottish psalms, I liked the plainness, the role of the laity and (above all) the meaty, scholarly preaching. That tradition suited me for some twenty years, during which I got married, went to work for the BBC and dragged my wife and four children round the world as a foreign correspondent.

You see a lot of distressing things in that kind of job. During the 1960s I witnessed a great deal of violence – assassinations, riots, and the war in Vietnam (which was so brutal and so cynical). Churchgoing became intolerable; I had attacks of giddiness there as I looked up at the figure on the cross, it said only '*You* did this to me – and there is no health in you'. My religion was of no help, for if you have a sick mind, you will have a sick faith, too. In all the experience I have had since of counselling people with my condition, I have never known anybody *pray* their way out of depression – though religious people feel they ought to, and feel all the worse when they are unable to do so.

To cut a painful story short: soon after returning to London from the United States, I had a screaming nervous collapse. My doctor slammed on the brakes with a powerful tranquillizer which made me feel as if I were living in a thick glass case; then he sent me off to a classic Viennese psychiatrist and I lay there on the couch talking my head off – to stop him asking awkward questions.

The talking therapy is hard work. You have to do it all yourself and you get (deliberately) no sympathy from the psychiatrist. But in the end I sorted out all the old yearnings and resentments and confusions – things done for the best of motives but gone wrong and misunderstood. Above all, I learned about forgiveness – most of all, forgiving oneself – and about the desperate need we all have to be able to *give* love (even more than receive it) and so to accept oneself as loving and lovable and so forgivable. You will see at once that the message of forgiveness was what I had missed on the cross all the time.

But I found it now. My Damascus road was the street where my secular Jewish psychiatrist lived. And what he was telling me was what I was hearing at last in my new church, the Religious Society of Friends – the Quakers.

I had known a few Quakers in the past and admired them. In America my children attended a Quaker school, whose humanity we all respected. In my personal crisis with violence, the pacifism of the Quakers was attractive. And there was something more. It dawned upon me in the busy, talkative services of the mainstream churches: what did we think we were doing pestering God for favours, telling him how great he was, *who* he was, what he ought to do next – all of which he presumably knew already? Why did we not shut up and listen – in case he had something to say? I suppose the ancient mystical tradition was calling. As one great fourteenth-century English mystic put it: 'Clear your minds, I beg you, of your good thoughts as well as your bad ones and think only that you are as you are and He is as He is' – which, I suppose, is what Quakers try to do in their worship.

So I joined them, and found them full of recovered depressives like myself; not terribly interested in elaborate doctrine (doctrine, I think, is a tool to work with, a rope to help us climb the mountain – not an image to be worshipped for itself); seeking the direct experience of God in everyday life and work, perhaps a little too eager to approach human nature from the end of original goodness rather than original sin.

Well, it is not my purpose to make propaganda for the Quakers, passionately though I love them. Our founder, George Fox, thought that we would become the universal Church of the future – but it has not worked out that way. We are constantly said to be influential beyond all proportion to our numbers, but there are still only 18,000 or so in this country, and I think we have to accept the fact that our silence and our apparent vagueness as to what we really believe (we do not actually like that word – it is too prescriptive, too authoritarian about things we cannot *know*) will continue to limit our growth. I see us as a lay order within the great Church of the sons and daughters of God, fond of experiment as well as experience, speaking the language of Christianity but not always meaning the same as the others do. We have a great liberty of faith, but we do expect one another to share and compare insights so that we generally arrive at a consensus; we do not apply any test or creed, and we never throw people out – we find that if they do not feel comfortable with us, they just go of their own accord. We never count votes on anything. We have no clergy; no set liturgy; no sacraments – not even a Communion service. What – no Communion when Christ himself ordained it? Well, it is partly a matter of history: Fox and his friends thought that Communion was being used to bully and blackmail people, and they would not have *anyone* saying who should and who should not have access to the Lord. But there are theological arguments, too: that Christ *is* come again amongst us, in person; that every meal, indeed all life, is a sacrament; that anyway, we prefer to wash people's feet. And we do not like things that divide people and demand rigid interpretations of what is going on.

Personally, I am glad to share other people's Communions if invited – though they should understand that I may not mean by it quite what they mean. In this spirit I have received Commnunion from Methodists, Anglicans, from a Roman Catholic abbot who knew very well what he was doing, and according to the lovely rite of the Church of South India, where you stand round in a circle and communicate one another.

No wonder some of my fellow Quakers regard me as a crypto-Anglican entryist – or perhaps a crypto-Presbyterian. For a while I am very happy in the Society of Friends and feed richly on its traditions, I know that I have brought with me in my pilgrim's pack bits and pieces picked up from other churches which I have stayed in – because I find them meaningful and because they are useful. I have even got some Catholic relics: I am rather fond of saints, I furtively light candles when I get the chance, and concepts like recollection and the informed conscience are very handy – but, as I say, as tools to work with.

And the same goes for Scripture. Fox knew his Bible very well indeed, but he declined to worship it, and saw it as being at the disposal and under the sovereignty of the Holy Spirit. Scripture was just dead words unless the Spirit within the reader illumined what it needed for its purposes. The whole question of 'Is the Bible true?' seems to me ridiculous and rather insulting to the Bible: it was not written as an encyclopaedia or a collection of law reports. My philosophy tutors would be convulsed at the notion of its being literally true, and I agree. But is it *misleading*? No. Does it contain mighty and eternal *truths?* Yes. We ignore it at our peril.

But I cannot see any systematic religion as encapsulating 'The Truth'; so it is not a bad idea to settle for one tradition of faith and develop that, rather than gallop off in all directions with no discipline. But the point of such a system is not to represent 'The Truth' in all its completeness, but to help us to organize, handle and pass on as much truth as we can manage – and I find it outrageous to pretend that we can manage the whole truth about God, any more than astronomy can manage the whole truth about the universe.

The six years which I spent as the BBC's religious affairs correspondent, I regarded as a genuine vocation and a chance to distil something of value from the life I had led before. The response to the work was amazing: it made me realize how many people there were who had a religious dimension to their lives but did not feel the institutional churches could speak to their condition. My success was the churches' failure; and this bothers me, not only because I am totally unqualified to meet it, but because a plastic guru like me is not worth one finger of a caring pastoral priest – the electronic 'Church of the air' is *no* church, because it is no community. It may have the privilege of supporting and serving the Church as an auxiliary, but it is no substitute for the Church: that Church is here, not in Broadcasting House and certainly not in some satellite-beam telly-evangelists from the American Bible belt.

So I keep stumbling on my pilgrimage. Let me conclude with some of the bees that keep buzzing in my bonnet as I go (they are mostly paradoxes, by the way, and they shocked that eminent logician Sir Freddy Ayer):

- God would not be the God that he is if we could prove that he was. God needs the atheist – he needs a way out of *having* to exist, He must be optional or we cannot love him.

- God has weakened himself in creating man. Man is lost without God; but God is lost without man.
- If Jesus was not God, he is now. And yet God is more than Jesus and Jesus knew it.
- Perhaps the resolution is this, that in Jesus, God was saying: 'I am like this. Indeed, I am so like this that, so far as you can ever understand, I *am* this.'
- For me, the most startling verse in the Bible is that phrase in St John's gospel where Mary Magdalen meets the risen Christ and it says 'She, supposing him to be the gardener . . .'. He had become the gardener; a man on the road to Emmaus; a man by the lake grilling fish. . . . He had become everyman, everywoman, us.
- Jesus did not say 'Your sins will be forgiven'. He kept saying 'Your sins *are* forgiven'. But we cannot believe it.
- God loves you now – just as you are. But you cannot believe that, either.
- Crucifixion and resurrection were not once for all – they are now, and they are always. Actually, it should be Gethsemane, crucifixion and resurrection – they are the inseparable trio and you cannot have one without the others.
- The day we put God in a box, the world will come to an end.

Part of an address given to an Open University Seminar at the Centre for the Study of Theology, University of Essex, in May 1988.

The Church and the World

2

Margaret Thatcher as theologian

After years of attacking the clergy for talking politics, politicians have started dabbling in theology. Personally I have no objection at all to this. But if so, the politicians will now have to take the rough and tumble of hermeneutics like the rest of us.

It all began, as I remember, with an interview with Mrs Thatcher by a women's magazine, in which she accused the Church of letting the nation down morally. Then she went up to Edinburgh and preached at length to the General Assembly of the Church of Scotland, on the text of the Protestant work ethic.

Well, I shall follow the Prime Minister's career as a theologian with interest, but I fear she will have to do better next time. She recognizes, quite correctly, that you cannot keep faith and works in separate boxes. But the point of that, as I see it, is to keep the two hand in hand and not to let one of them – works, in her case – go bounding away over the horizon. The Prime Minister also recognizes that you do not have to be a Christian to do right, but she believes that Christians are impelled towards it by certain spiritual essentials of which she identifies three. Would grace, perhaps, be one of them? Curiously not. Two concern individual moral choice and responsibility, while the third is the sacrifice of Christ in order that our sins might be forgiven. Now I think that points in the right direction and it is said to be basic simple Christianity. But I do not find it simple myself; it has bothered me for ages. So I would like to know what the Prime Minister really understands by the Atonement, and I hope she will tell us soon.

Mrs Thatcher goes on to quote, with approval, a certain preacher saying 'No one took away the life of Jesus. He chose to lay it down.' Well, at Gethsemane there *was* a choice; but we are not talking about a suicide. Have we – collectively – no responsibility for his crucifixion, which still goes on? If not, what is all this fuss about sin and repentance and forgiveness?

The Prime Minister proceeds through the Ten Commandments and the ethic of Do-as-you-would-be-done-by. But I am worried about this emphasis on morality as the heart of the Christian faith. Christianity is not fundamentally about being good. Of course Christians are expected to behave rightly, like anyone else; but at its heart the faith is about things like creation, incarnation, crucifixion, resurrection, forgiveness, worship, prayer. Salvation is a tricky concept for me; but as I understand it the key questions at our justification will not be 'Did you create wealth? Did you stretch yourself?' but 'Did you serve your brothers and sisters? Did you feed the hungry, clothe the naked, visit the sick and oppressed?' Here and there, the Prime Minister indicates that she knows this. But her emphasis keeps returning to individual responsibility for choosing what is right and doing what is good, almost as if there were no social environment, no political framework, no economic order, no groups or classes which help to condition and define the individual. To analyse life in terms of individual choice is to oversimplify it grotesquely.

The Prime Minister (who took office quoting St Francis) is now quoting St Paul: 'If a man will not work he shall not eat.' But what is to happen to the hundreds of thousands of men and women who cannot find work? May we not, in the exercise of our right of individual choice, commission the State to help them on our behalf? Is that so wrong? Is that unreasonable? Old Testament and New are not just concerned with individual self-salvation (any more than they are solely concerned with the life to come). Both are also about community – the community of Israel and its rulers, the community of the early Christian Church and its oppressors. The Church itself is a community – or a community of communities. Christ spoke constantly to larger and smaller groups of followers, commanding them to get together and love one another – which is to care for one another. To inherit eternal life we must love God and our neighbour – not just ourself.

There are grave dangers in individualized – dare I say 'privatized?' – faith. At best it is complacent, selfish and shallow;

at worst, it can go mad and become positively evil. The Church is by no means impeccable in this respect, but it does have its discipline; it provides an orthodoxy against which the heretic must prove his case; and it is not built on two thousand years of collective folly.

The assertion of 'absolute moral values' (to quote the Prime Minister) seems an example of theological shallowness. By all means 'assert' love, mercy and courage; but in the real situations of the people it is about as effective as 'condemning' violence, cruelty, hatred. And what then? There is no such thing as an abstract moral question; there are only particular cases. And it is in the nature of a moral dilemma that it occurs where two or more issues conflict. How can you resolve a moral dilemma by ruling that one absolute value is more absolute than another? Instead, you have to employ casuistry (in its true sense) and give one value priority over another for reasons of your own, depending upon the sort of person you define yourself as being. There is plenty of room for Thatcherite choice and responsibility there; but do not imagine that your decisions will be beyond controversy or reproach. The Ten Commandments board will not solve all your problems at a glance; time and again you will need to turn to some collective and its traditions for guidance.

If Christianity has a special contribution to make in the moral sphere, it is not 'How to be good' but 'How to cope with sin and failure and wickedness'. In an increasingly complex and difficult society – and that is part of the trouble today: there are so many decisions and choices to be made and so much confusing information upon which to base them – you are not going to make people more virtuous by rubbing their noses in 'absolute moral values'.

* * *

The Prime Minister's lead was shortly followed by an article in the *Church Times* from the Home Secretary, Douglas Hurd, calling upon the Churches to pull their weight in the fight against crime and immorality; in his view, the Church was uniquely placed to provide the nation with moral leadership. 'That authority', he declared, 'rests firmly with the Church.'

Alas, the Church today is very *badly* placed, and its authority is most *infirm*. The criminal classes do not come to church to hear sermons on the Ten Commandments or anything else, and the days are long gone when Bishop Wilson of Sodor and Man could throw drunkards and adulterers into his episcopal jail and have unmarried mothers dragged across Peel Harbour at a rope's end. (He was, we are told, much loved by his people, nevertheless.) If the Church has lost its moral police powers, that is partly the fault of the State, which took them away for its own use, substituting the concept of crime for that of sin.

Why the Church has lost the attention of the people is a long and complicated question which goes back at least two centuries and has nothing to do with the Bishop of Durham, women's ordination or the declining use of the 1662 Prayer Book. I am sure the decline has been accelerated by the sheer growth of counter-attractions, from TV, gardening and motoring to the enormous size of Sunday newspapers. More fundamental is the loss of useful function: the Church is no longer responsible for education, welfare, scholarship and the arts, nor has it an acknowledged place in our social hierarchy. Few people are impressed any more by threats of plague or hell fire. Above all, in my opinion, the Church waited too long before taking up the challenges of science and of history. Two World Wars found it with nothing convincing to say about God, human cruelty and the suffering of the innocent (as if incarnation, crucifixion and resurrection did not go to the heart of these matters). And instead of welcoming the revelations of science as extending God's glory, the Church mumbled with embarrassment and tried to pretend it was talking about some other universe.

However, ministers of the present government seem to want it both ways when it comes to the Church. On the one hand they want the Church to make the people behave – behave in their secular life. On the other, they want the Church to keep its hands off the secular world, and complain when it tries to teach by suggesting what might actually be done. For here comes the Education Secretary, Mr Kenneth Baker, back on the old line that (to quote *The Times*) 'parts of the Church of England seemed to have become absorbed with secular concerns and social policies, with clergymen seeing themselves purely as social workers'. Purely? I suppose feeding the hungry, sheltering the homeless, clothing the naked and the rest *could* be described as social work; and when you think of all the healing and counselling he did, our Lord may count as a social worker. But was this merely secular in significance?

To quote Mr Baker further, he thinks 'It was no coincidence that those parts of the church enjoying the greatest support were those concerning themselves with personal salvation' and that 'churches which seek relevance by involving themselves overly with secular concerns only alienate those who have turned to them in the hope of finding traditional values and spiritual certainties'.

Now, I do not think there are a lot of spiritual *certainties* (I could wish there were, but perhaps it is the *un*certainty that is so stimulating). And while traditional values sound fine, we still have to figure out how they apply to particular cases and crises. Mr Baker is obviously impressed by born-again evangelical Christianity and its enthusiasm for personal commitment to Jesus – and if that speaks to your condition, good luck to you, say I. But it does not speak to everyone, and some of us would say it is only a beginning, and possibly a false one if it does not lead to a wider and deeper spiritual life.

But then the whole background to Church/State relations in Britain is confusing. The Church of England has always been deeply involved in politics, so why should it stop now? You have only to think of figures like Henry VIII, Elizabeth I, James II and William of Orange, to see what I mean. And it remains the official, established Church of the State, subject still to the ultimate control of Parliament. But of course it is no longer the Tory Party at prayer – or if it is, it is the Tory Party of yesteryear and not today. And this is bewildering to the new radical Toryism.

As I observed earlier, the Church always used to combine social, educational and other works with its spiritual functions. It then converted the State to the duty of taking these over, not least because far bigger resources were called for than the Church could command. But it has never lost an instinct for them – how could it, with the gospel prompting it? – and today it is aware of what is being left undone, and making a fuss about it. Government does not like that, and it particularly dislikes being criticized by a large, independent source of comment which (after all) has some experience in these matters and has its agents all over the country who know, or should know, what the people are going through.

It is very tiresome for Government – which thinks that it alone knows the facts and carries the burdens – to be told that it is wrong. But the State does need independent sources of criticism, and now that it is seeking to trivialize or destabilize the mass media, it is important that the Churches should not lose their nerve, should not retreat into piety and personal salvation. I was very glad to see the Prime Minister, in her Scottish homily, emphasizing the importance of tolerance, courtesy and mutual respect. They may not be qualities much in evidence in the lives of the Prophets or on the benches of the House cf Commons; but I do find it one of the more distressing features of the political scene that so many people in power hate to hear things they disagree with. Does not individual choice extend to letting people choose what to believe and what not to believe? Yet you might think that the Bishop of Durham had been leading the mob in burning down police stations rather than discussing traditional doctrines in a rather old-fashioned way. As, indeed have I.

Address first given at an Open University Seminar, University of Essex, in May 1988 and revised for Hull Divinity Seminar the following December; the text combines passages from both versions.

3

The Church of the future

'The Church of the Future' is both a hard subject and a soft one. Hard because the one thing certain about history is that it is inscrutable. Soft because, by the time this future we are speaking of comes about, few of you will remember what I say, anyway.

I suppose the best course is to start from where we are now and to see which way things are pointing – to take a very short-range view of the future. What are the growing-points? You may say that there are none; that over all, every index is in decline. But this is not altogether true: some churches may be dying, but others are coming alive. If you look at figures like the sale of religious books and the audiences for religious broadcasting, there is a rising tide of interest in religious matters, even if people are shy of joining religious institutions. It is the Church which is under challenge, not God; and as the population grows older, I would expect this to become more marked. People look for a meaning in their lives, past and future, and regret that the Church has not supplied it.

Yet I believe that we need the Church; and I see many dangers in privatized, introspective, unorganized religion. So where, in the institutional Church, can we see signs of life?

Well, there is the ecumenical movement – the coming together of denominations both nationally and internationally – and there is great busy-ness in this area. Within this country there is certainly an evangelical revival, and to a lesser extent an Anglo-Catholic response. Both may be seen as reactions to an earlier wave of liberal and progressive churchmanship; though I have to say that, English theology being rather a backwater, that wave was not really so progressive by American or Continental standards. In fact, it was rather old-fashioned: middle-of-the-road rather than liberal.

But it did help to throw up such developments as the movement for the ordination of women, the modern English services, the engagement in social affairs, and the synodical government of the Church of England – all of them stimulants or irritants according to your taste. And this has brought in another factor which I fancy will make itself increasingly felt: the re-engagement of the State in the affairs of the Church, and more particularly the official national church (the Church of England) which still remains ultimately subject to Parliament and hence to the Government.

Since 1927, when it rejected the revision of the Prayer Book, Parliament has not shown much interest in exercising that control. That is one reason why synodical government by the Church's own parliament arose. But hear the words of that noted churchman, Mr Enoch Powell: 'The essential nature of the Church of England is not doctrinal but political'; and over the past few years we have heard growing complaints that the Synod has been usurping the powers of Parliament.

First, there was resentment in Government ranks over the Synod passing resolutions critical of state policy on housing, unemployment, social security payments, immigration and so forth. Then, just two years ago, Mr John Gummer – a cabinet minister as well as a member of Synod – played the parliamentary card during a debate on women's ordination: reminding Synod that whatever it might decide was subject to House of Commons veto. Now there is an organized movement in both chambers of Parliament to call the Church of England to heel.

Today, after a period when the Church was castigated for getting into politics, politicians are leaping into the affairs of the Church with gusto. The Prime Minister delivers a homily on the Protestant work ethic to the Church of Scotland. The Home Secretary calls on Synod to help fight crime by asserting the Ten Commandments (though, alas, burglars and rapists are not on the whole regular churchgoers). The Secretary of State for Education reprimands the Church for neglecting the teaching of morality: will the Church kindly tell the people to behave themselves?

All this seems to me (as it does to the present Archbishop of Canterbury) a thoroughly healthy development for both sides and wonderful publicity for God. If the politicians want to get involved in theology, they are welcome, so long as they do not seek to lay down the law for the rest of us. The Church, for its part, must make the politicians realize that its concern over things like poverty, unemployment, homelessness and racism is not just trendy secular fashion but is rooted in Christian concepts like creation, incarnation, redemption and grace. Christianity is about much more than orderly behaviour and wealth creation. The key question at our judgement (we are told) will be 'Did you serve my children – who are me?'

The primary purpose of the Church is not to make people good, but to help them to know God, to love God and to worship him. Righteousness follows from that, not from moralizing. In any case, sin and crime are not synonymous: there are no laws against envy, greed, extravagance or lack of compassion, although to the Church they are timeless evils. And pastoral clergy know very well that people's moral choices are not made in a vacuum but under many pressures, including those generated by Government.

So the Church of the future will have to back its social concerns with spiritual conviction. I think it will also have to ordain women, in spite of the kicking and screaming; and that by the turn of the century we shall all be wondering what the fuss was about. To me it seems ridiculous – but then, what else would you expect of a Quaker? There will probably be some schism, but a great deal less than has been threatened; for a noisy war of nerves is being waged, largely with blank ammunition.

Will it mean a setback to the ecumenical process? Will it, in particular, alienate Rome? To some extent it must. But I think the ground that has been gained in recent years will be held, and any that seems lost will be largely imaginary.

What has been gained in the past forty years is charity, friendship, courtesy and hospitality amongst the Churches, at all levels, to a degree unthinkable in the past. Quietly, and maybe irregularly, intercommunion between Romans and others has become quite common. There is no need to lose this. But if Rome still cannot recognize the validity of the Anglican priesthood as it is now, what difference can it make if women are ordained? It is hard to imagine the present Pope, or the kind of men who seem likely to succeed him, modifying their stand on this point. This is not to say that Anglican/Roman Catholic theological dialogue is a waste of time; I just do not believe that any sort of merger or submission has ever been on the cards or is waiting in the pack.

In any case, would it increase the glory of God to reduce the variety of our perceptions and celebrations of him? Having been in three denominations myself, I cannot see it in this way. I am bound to have a certain respect for the pilgrim who, honestly responding to his or her experience, moves on from one tradition to another, grateful to each for what it has given and keeping something precious from each. In my Father's house are many apartments and we are not required, I think, to crowd into a single dormitory. We are required, however, to be good neighbours to one another.

So I have to say that I hope the Church of the future will not be less varied than it is today, apart from a little tidying up where it makes practical sense. We all see God from where we stand – from where he has seen fit to place us – and this means that we are bound to take different views of him, and should be cautious before denouncing anyone else's as wrong. The Bible Protestant has one perspective; the sacramental Catholic another; the mystic a third; the existentialist a fourth. No one believer can be all of these but we can each try to understand and respect the others, and I believe that they add up to a fuller (though still imperfect) image of the one God.

Thus, it is something more like a federal rather than a united 'Church of the churches' that I foresee; though I am bound to say, also, that I am apprehensive about the complicated structure of so-called Ecumenical Instruments that the British Council of Churches is working on at the moment. In my experience, the Holy Spirit seldom attends committee meetings, and God draws up his own timetable and agenda.

We have tried the legislative and treaty-making approach to unity before – twice between Anglicans and Methodists, and again with the so-called 'covenanting process' – and it has not worked. In any case, when two churches unite the end result is invariably three: the united body and two residual or 'continuing' churches. This is the familiar story of any denomination in the United States where, incidentally, no one thinks any the worse of it. Indeed, compared with England, it is an intensely churchgoing country. Perhaps we need more denominations, not less; perhaps it would stimulate piety if the Church of England did split, and stopped trying to be all things to all men – although bringing it about, like Disestablishment, would be a legislative, financial and administrative nightmare.

Or shall we, perhaps, abandon the church of the gothic arches and take to the church of the air – the church of the satellite, the TV screen and the 'telly-evangelist'? I devoutly hope not: religious broadcasting can be an auxiliary or supplement to the Church, but it cannot be a substitute for it. For a start, it cannot administer any sacrament. It has no rigour or discipline. It has no community of people who are obligated to love and serve one another. And a dozen telly-evangelists are not worth one single pastoral priest or minister; the church of the air is, in my opinion, a phoney church.

As a matter of observation rather than recommendation, I cannot think of any religious movement which has expanded successfully without at least two of three things. The first, which is essential, is a clear cut doctrine: to be able to say, this we believe, this we teach. Second and third, you need one or both of the following: at least one dominant preacher like Fox, like Wesley, like Smith of the Mormons, like L. Ron Hubbard, Sun Myung Moon, the Maharishi and Dr Ian Paisley; and/or a dedicated cadre of missionaries. But today in Britain we have none of these (apart from Dr Paisley) and, with some reason, we are suspicious of them all.

When all is said and done, it is the Holy Spirit which will decide the Church of the future. And for all I know, the Spirit will decide to scatter the churches, let them die, and start all over again. It may, for example, force us to get our noses out of the trough of man-made doctrine and dogma, liturgy and hierarchy, and look to our stewardship of God's first gift to us – creation itself, or as the secular world now calls it, the environment. Perhaps we shall be compelled to a new form of nature worship.

But this is not something that leaps from the pages of the Bible as it stands. Care for the environment can easily be justified from Scripture, but it was not one of the preoccupations of our Lord or St Paul, any more than they gave us guidance on birth control or euthanasia or genetic engineering. Many of the moral concerns of Christians today have been forced upon them by secular and scientific pressures, not by the explicit commands of Scripture. And this has always been so: that somebody interprets the faith in the context of the times and in the language of the times. The results may be disturbing – especially for those who are comfortable with yesterday's reading of it, and who denounce the updating as mere trendiness. But *is* Christianity a way of life – a way of living today – or is it just an unchanging ritual, a holy gesture?

Trusting as I do in the love of God – that he wills our welfare and not our destruction – I look to the Church of the future for a renewal of prophecy and preaching. As always, some of it will be false, and much of it will be vainly and tediously fundamentalist. But all through the history of the Church, it has been the personal voice, the personal example, that has affirmed the will of God and converted the people. Such personal examples used to be called saints; and that is what they are, even when the title is not bestowed officially. We should look out for them, test them and cherish them. And I assure you, they will not all be wearing dog-collars.

The Church of the future, I think, will demand far more of its lay people than it gets today. The successful church will be (already is) the one that harnesses their devotion. Indeed, most of the churches today are begging the laity to come forward and assume greater responsiblity. But the attitude of 'leave it to the Reverend – let Father do it' dies hard.

I have said it all depends on the Holy Spirit. But the Holy Spirit can act through no body but yours. The Church of the future is you. What do you want to make of it?

Sermon preached at Hertford College, Oxford, on 12 February 1989.

4

The churches – a problem of long division

Every year, all over England, Christians meet to pay quite literally, and even sincerely, lip-service to the ideal of Christian unity. St John's Gospel tells us that Jesus prayed 'that they all may be one' – that Jesus wanted us to be one. But do we really want to be one?

I do not think we do; I am quite sure that I do not, if it means Baptists becoming Roman Catholics and Presbyterians turning Anglican – what a loss of richness that would be! If that is what Jesus meant, most of us, in our heart of hearts, would beg to differ. Most of us would be baffled at the prospect of serving the Lord's will by betraying our own understanding of it.

But how could Jesus have meant that? In Christ there was neither Baptist nor Presbyterian, Orthodox nor Catholic. Before I am dragged from this rostrum and burnt at the stake, I had better define a few terms; and I had better begin by trying to tell you where I start from personally.

I am a member of the Society of Friends – the Quakers – a very small group of Christians, not more than 20,000 in this country, founded in the middle of the seventeenth century (the age of *The Pilgrim's Progress*) in protest against the efforts of the Church to erect barriers between God and humanity – or that is how it seemed to the early Friends and their leader, George Fox. Creeds, forms of service, the Thirty-nine Articles, the Westminster Confession, the ordained priesthood itself were all seen as unlawful attempts to define God and to say who was and who was not worthy to approach him. The Quakers were a profoundly biblical people. They insisted they were not inventing a new religion but, like all reformers, claimed that they were getting back to the original, uncontaminated faith of the Apostles.

Whether they were doing so or not, I cannot say; I am not

sure that we can ever tell what the original faith of the apostles really was. We do know, however, that what mattered to the early Quakers was that their own spiritual experience should bring the gospel alive: the Scriptures themselves were dead – it was useless to repeat them – unless one had experienced their truth within. And this could only be achieved not by looking outwards to some altar or preacher, but by looking deep into oneself where the Inward Light of Christ himself was to be found in each one of us.

Friends did *not* make the mistake of treating their faith and worship as a purely private matter for the individual. They knew that madness and self-deception can lie that way – as sometimes it did for Friends. They insisted upon the sharing and mutual criticism of revelation, upon subjecting such ministry as might come to them to the prayerful contemplation of the Meeting, and its correction (if need be) in the light of the Society's traditions. But at the root of it all, Quakers believed, and still believe, that everyone may have direct access to God in silent worship, without human intermediary, and without passing any test of faith. Quakers are, I would say, a contemplative order within the one great Church that encompasses all Christians; though since we do not practise the use of any sacrament (not even that of the Lord's Supper) nor require subscription to the doctrine of the Trinity, some of you may think we are not Christians at all. We mildly beg to differ.

As a result of my labours over the past year, I am perhaps more tolerant of your ways than you might be of mine. For though I remain devotedly a Quaker, I think I now see the point of doctrine, of sacraments, of the Church itself, in a way that may help us all towards an understanding of Christian unity which is not self-defeating by being exclusive. For surely, if all are to be one, we must try not to shut each other out – and I am even more anxious to let into the churches those who are totally outside them, than I am to merge those who are already within. That, surely, is the even greater task that lies before us.

Let me take first the stumbling-block of the priesthood or ordained ministry. Some might say that Matthew 23 – 'Be not ye called Rabbi . . . all ye are brethren . . . call no man your father upon the earth . . .' – shows our Lord actually prohibiting such a role; and indeed, we know that some branches of the early

Church drew lots among the laity at every service, to see who should preside, who preach, who read the Scriptures, so that there was no permanent priesthood. Quakers try to minister mutually to one another. But it seems to me that, quite apart from sacramental considerations, most congregations do feel the need of a fixed leadership and of the teaching authority of some person trained and studied in the traditions of the Church. He or she must be the chief servant of all; and I would be the first to recognize that a devoted pastor who truly cares for the flock is worth a score of media gurus like myself, tossing out mere words without having to come to grips with their meaning in human situations.

The Church, of course, is all of us, and by no means limited to the priesthood and its hierarchy, who would agree with me that they are its least important members; and we need the Church, above all, to keep alive the stories about God. Essentially this means the Bible and its stories, and there are those who say 'Why do we need the Church when we have the Bible: surely the whole Christian truth is to be seen there in all its simplicity?' I must disagree with this for two reasons: first, that the Bible is *not* simple. How could it be, when it was written over many centuries from many different points of view – the latest of them almost two thousand years away from our culture and in modes of thought which are very different from our own? I have found very few, even among the most Bible-based Christians, who will deny that the Bible needs constant interpretation and scholarship if it is to be understood aright and not merely be used to confirm our private assumptions. The Church is the repository of generations of experience in those arts. Odd that it should be necessary to say this, but we should remember that throughout the Dark Ages, the Middle Ages, the Renaissance period and well into the nineteenth century, the best minds of Western Christendom were at the service of the Church; even the great secular philosophers exercised their minds within the Christian framework, and it is a sign of arrogance (as well as ignorance) to despise them.

My second reason for asserting that the Church is essential to the Bible is that those very stories are fragile and defenceless things; they need preserving and protecting, as well as publishing abroad. In every age there have been attempts to improve upon the Bible by curious and heretical versions of it. That is not to say that modern scholarship cannot sometimes clarify the texts we have, or that the King James version (which was not actually dictated by the Almighty, as some people appear to think) is perfect; but any improvements have to be subjected to rigorous examination, and for that too I think we need the Church.

So, since it holds this treasure in its hands, we need the Church to teach, tell and celebrate the stories about God. For if the Church does not do this, there is a real danger of their dying, and these stories – far more than the doctrines derived from them – are the heart of the Christian faith. Jesus himself taught in stories, both in the parables he told and in the things he did which became stories. And the marvellous thing about stories is that they are always human, always about people (rather than laws or theories) and they are open-ended: they go on, they lead somewhere – often to another story. We owe that to the Jewish origins of our faith.

We need the Church, too – as Quakers need their Meetings – as a critic of our private revelations. Many people – far more than you may think – have a private religious life of their own: they receive messages, they experience apprehensions of the infinite, they work out theories about God and electricity, or construct graphs showing how this world and the next are connected – and then they send them to me! There are times when I think that this is not a godless country at all, but a nation of amateur theologians.

Now I would say, as any Quaker must, that without personal experience of God, all professions of faith are worthless. But we know that unless exposed to the criticism and tests of the community – which includes the wisdom of its traditions – private revelation can be mistaken.

Very often, too, it is selfish or commonplace. People arrive at the conclusion that they must keep themselves pure, or that loving one another is all that matters. But how? And what then? What about sin? What about suffering, failure and evil? At its worst, private revelation can lead us into evil, to the mass suicide of Mr Jones and his followers in Guyana, or to the Yorkshire Ripper claiming to murder prostitutes at God's command.

So we have evidence of what can happen when people

persuade themselves that the Church is optional or unnecessary, and cut themselves off from it or construct a selective church of their own. The Church can only represent God to man and man to God when it is at its widest, when it collects and concentrates the rays shining from above and below.

We need the Church also to remind us that the Christian faith has always been a matter of community, not of private salvation. Christianity involves belonging to a society of friends for whom we have to care – that is what loving one another really means – whether we actually like one another very much or not. To love your neighbour as yourself does not mean to find somebody you love and go to bed with them; it means to care for anyone you bump into. That is the story of the Good Samaritan.

And what about doctrine – those hoary old superstitions that reasonable people know we have outgrown – including the doctrine of the Trinity, which I used to compare rather frivolously to the Victorian piano in the front parlour, which nobody plays any more, but nobody can bring themselves to throw out?

I think it was St Augustine who described doctrine as 'only an alternative to silence'. He meant that either we give up trying to say the unsayable, and say nothing (which is rather what Quakers do), or we say something inadequate and provisional. We do not pretend (or should not) that the doctrine of the Trinity provides a blueprint from which we can build a replica of God. It simply tells us that God is not a static mass of holiness, but a dynamic system of activity and relationships: God the Father 'up there', as it were; God the Son 'down here' with us; and the Holy Spirit as the spark dancing between them. I am persuaded that although you will not find the Trinity worked out in the New Testament, nevertheless it was a reasonable construction from the experience of the early Church. From their Jewish origins they knew of God the Father; the Son was a historical figure in their midst; and although he had been taken from them, his Spirit was still undeniably at work amongst them.

Doctrine like this is just a way of trying to package up vital information, putting brown paper around it, so that it does not fall apart and blow away. Or looked at another way, it is a hard wall of consensus off which heretics like me can bounce our ideas, the orthodoxy against which any reformer must prove his case, just as in the world of science, no new discovery is taken seriously unless it can take on the old system in its own terms. Once more, doctrine is a set of tools with which we can shape the shapeless mass of experience that confronts us; a set of ropes and climbing-irons with which we attempt to climb the mountain. Doctrine is to be used, not worshipped.

And sacraments? Sacraments, it seems to me, are 'another language'. They are ways of saying things that cannot otherwise be said. But they are not just ways in which the priest or the Church presents mysteries to the people; they are a language which God uses to speak to us all. For we must never forget that religion is not magic. It is not something we do in order to manipulate God – not smoke signals that we send up, hoping the Big Chief in the Skies will see them and favour us. True religion is two-way: it is much more a matter of God seeking to manipulate us, and of our responding to him. The 'wishful thinking' theory of religion does not work because if, for all these thousands of years, mankind had just been chanting, sacrificing and gesticulating at nothing, the pantomime would long since have been abandoned. It only goes on because we know that there is something coming back in the opposite direction. There is a response; or rather, it is we who respond to God's initiative, and there are many who find that initiative in the sacramental life of the Church.

For myself, I think the whole of life is sacramental, a visible token of God's love for us, which demands our response to complete it (as love always does). But I confess this is not an easy frame of mind to get into; and I can see the appeal of summing up the divine grace in these special moments of ritual like Holy Communion, Baptism, Marriage, Confession. We may differ as to precisely what goes on in the bread and wine; but even a Quaker can acknowledge that, for the faithful communicant, it is far more than 'just' bread and wine.

Now what I have said about the life of the institutional churches, their ministry, doctrine and sacraments, must fall short of how you see yourselves, and can have done little to suggest how you might come closer to each other. I doubt if it has done anything to make a Free Church member readier to accept bishops, nor an Anglican readier to accept papal infallibility, nor a Roman Catholic to share the Eucharist with either. And what a reproach it is to sacramental Christians in general when that

Eucharist – the very central expression of the faith – is apparently the very last thing they can share! Let me warn you – what you may know already – that there are guerrillas in your midst who cannot wait for formal agreements on these matters and are already sharing the bread and wine, regardless of canon law, with or without an ordained priest, in their homes and offices. I am absolutely convinced that this will grow, whatever the hierarchies may say; just as I am convinced that the priesthood of women will spread. It is not for me either to instigate or deplore this: it is simply what I see happening, and it seems to me that the institutional churches will have to decide whether unity and truth require them to discipline these practices or embrace them. It may be hard to kick against the pricks; but who is wielding them, and where are they trying to drive us?

I have to confess that although I love you all as brothers and sisters under the one Father, you folk are not, at this stage in my life, the principal object of my concern. You have your structures and ceremonies, and have been negotiating earnestly through covenants, councils and commissions, and I wish you every success. If it is of vital importance to you whether the Eucharist is a sacrifice or a memorial, and whether your leaders are validly in the apostolic succession or not, then it is certainly not for me to persuade you otherwise. It is almost beside the point, I suppose, what our Lord would have made of such issues. I sometimes wonder if he would have been accepted for ordination, let alone his disciples.

What I am deeply concerned about (because they are the people who speak to me in a constant stream of letters and conversation) is what I call 'the great anonymous church of the unchurched' – the people who *would be* Christians (and I think often are) but who will not come near the churches because of what they perceive the churches to be: still obsessed with the forms and formalities of the past, but disapproving of the ordinary, intelligent person's doubts and experiences. In other words, they find you shut, not open. Now these people are often wide open in their honesty and integrity. They may not be very well informed about what the Christian faith can be – poor souls, how are they to get the information these days, especially if they never come to church? But openness of their kind was something our Lord valued most highly.

As I have said, private religion is often narrow and mistaken. That is inevitable when people cut themselves off, or feel cut off, from the Church; for the Church is often wider than these outsiders realize. In all my conversations with leading churchmen over the past year, I have found them more flexible, more open to development (more progressive, dare I say?), than I had ever expected. But the outsiders do not know this, or are not convinced of it. Sometimes they have had frightening experiences of one of the narrower sects, and to them the Church still teaches a code of unreasonable certainties, instead of (what I believe to be the case) a code of reasonable uncertainties.

The Church badly needs such people to counteract the sterile secularism of our times; and I believe such people need the Church, for the reasons I gave earlier – though it may be a Church in a different shape from what we have now. Maybe there should be mergers, covenants, ecumenical ministries, shared buildings and all the rest. You may have noticed that throughout this address I have been talking of 'the Church' without specifying which of many, as if there already was 'one Church' – as, in a sense, I believe there already is: the one great Church of the children of Christ.

It is my experience of the Inward Light that God speaks to each one of us in the language appropriate to each. You may say it is an accident that one is born a Catholic, another a Methodist, a third a Hindu – though I fancy that, to a Christian, accident is hardly the word; it would certainly not be to a Hindu. I think it would be a tragedy and a betrayal if the churches were to interpret the words 'that they all may be one' in a restricted ecclesiastical sense, as though Christ was praying 'that Catholics and Protestants may all agree on the theology of the Eucharist'. I doubt if that will happen, and I dare to say it does not matter. What does matter is that all who call themselves Christians should feel able to come within the great Church (in which I include my own Society – a quiet side chapel within the great cathedral), should feel able to work together and, on occasions more frequent than this, to worship together; and that their differences – or I would rather say, their variety – should be seen not to matter compared with the question 'do they love one another?' Or, in less sentimental terms, 'do they care for one another and for their neighbours?'

It is not entirely the fault of the churches that there are so many outside. I am not sure that this ever was a terribly pious country, and today the counter-attractions of the secular world and the lack of stillness make it hard for the voice of religion to make itself heard. But I do think that the Church has helped to cut itself off from people's lives, as well as being cut off; and that the separation has been at two levels, social and intellectual.

On the social level one can hardly regret that the State now concerns itself with the education, welfare work, medical care and sponsorship of the arts that were once the almost exclusive interest of the Church. It was once the Church that provided the schools, universities, hospices, hospitals, festivals and libraries which we now expect from government. The Church, of course, no longer has the money, the government having removed it from your pockets and mine. But this has meant that quite apart from losing the opportunities for evangelizing, the Church has lost many of the opportunities it had for showing Chrisitanity in action as a working, serving part of society. Yet opportunities still exist, and I wish that the churches had the courage (and the funds) to win back some of their lost territory, to occupy some of the neglected no man's land. Somebody had better do so, if cuts in services are going to continue, and we are to have (as seems probable) a permanent reservoir of two or three million unemployed.

The Church has also become separated from society at the intellectual level. A colleague of mine pointed out the other day that this is a danger to which Protestanism has always been susceptible – and, if I may say so, English Protestantism in particular, for we are a profoundly anti-intellectual nation; we do not like cleverness nor really respect education. The Catholic Church, going back to the early Fathers, Augustine and Aquinas, has a long tradition of reasoned philosophy, indistinguishable from theology. The Protestant Churches, on the other hand, have tended to reject intellectual Christianity and to emphasize faith, the conversion experience, above reason. Consequently they have been ill-equipped to stand up to the attacks of materialist science and politics. I think it is less and less true – if it ever was – that science is the enemy of religion. I find myself almost embarrassed by the number of scientists these days who seem to find themselves proving the existence of God. But this only brings me back to my point, that the churches – by their neglect of reasoned apologetics and theology and moral philosophy – have allowed religion to appear old-fashioned and unreasonable.

This is not to claim that you can prove the Christian faith by pure logic; it is heart and guts as well as head, and those you cannot move by reason alone. But it is not witless, and it is time that Christians stopped crying 'All you need is the simple faith that Jesus is Lord', girded up their intellectual loins, caught up with the secular thinking of the age, and tackled it on its own terms. For if the Church does not engage the bright young minds of our society, other institutions will, and they will lead us.

I am not calling for wild theological anarchy, but rather for great seriousness towards *those who are not here*. If everyone here tonight was to embrace in a single Church, ninety per cent of the community would still be outside. We would still not have answered our Lord's prayer 'that they *all* may be one'.

Talk delivered to Carshalton Council of Churches on 21 January 1982. The 'labours over the past year', including conversations with leading churchmen, were in connection with the BBC series *Priestland's Progress*, broadcast during 1981.

5

The quality of life – this world or the next?

This is not the first 'memorial lecture' I have given; and I must admit there have been times when I have wondered secretly whether the eponym and I really had anything in common. But on this occasion it is a perfect fit. I was brought up on encyclopaedias: they were my favourite reading from the age of five; and now the latest edition of the *Britannica* is literally within arm's reach of my writing-desk. Only today, I was rummaging through it in pursuit of 'parthenogenesis'. So I can heartily salute the memory of John Armitage.

Whether he would approve of the twist I have given to his theme 'the quality of life', is another matter; but then, it is a theme with so much mileage in it just because it can be given such twists. My starting point is this: when one hears the expression 'quality of life', one tends to start thinking of the environment, of architecture, social services, cultural activities – things of this world; but to the religious person, and especially the Christian, the further thought must occur: 'But this is a transitory life – are we not really here to prepare for something more lasting? Is there not a conflict between the qualities of this world and the next?'

So I want to consider the relationship between those worlds, and why we should bother about the one, or the other, or both. I admit to having a Christian bias in my approach; although I need hardly assure you it will not be an orthodox one!

That phrase 'quality of life' intrigues me, for a start, because the more I look at it, the less sure I am what it means. In one sense, I suppose, it stands in diametric contrast to 'quantity of life' or 'life that is quantifiable'. The implication is that we should stop our obsession with the gross national product, disposable incomes, productivity, balance of payments, live births per thousand and life expectation, and ask ourselves what is it all for, how is it spent? A rich ugly society, rolling in money but poisoned with violence and greed, is not worth having. And what shall it profit a man to live to the age of a hundred, if he is racked with pain and helpless with senility? The quantity of years does not guarantee the quality of life: that has become a rather specialized meaning of the phrase, and it has led some people to dabble in euthanasia. I am bound to say that while I have sympathy with anyone who feels driven down that road, I would lead them back from it if I could. To end life is no way to improve its quality.

But one also sees the phrase in a frankly hedonistic context: 'Enjoy the quality of life at Sunniclyffe Retirement Colony' says the brochure, and there it is – clock golf, gladioli, and a visiting chiropodist every Tuesday. Higher up the pleasure scale wait bungalows in the Channel Isles, with fitted carpets, cocktail cabinets and something called a Jacuzzi.

But no, not in Letchworth: everyone knows that here the quality of life is defined by chamber music recitals (no Bartok, please!), folk-dancing and macrobiotic food with lots of fibre. My *Encyclopaedia Britannica* (that part of it described as the Micropaedia) tells me the local industries include the production of corsets and baby-carriages, both calculated to enhance the quality of life. For 'enhancing' is what one does to it, just as 'boggling' is what one does to the mind.

The trouble is that no sooner do we take an oath to renounce mere quantity in favour of quality, than we find ourselves tempted to define quality in terms of quantity (or at least material measures) again. You can have the biggest Jacuzzi in the world and be miserable in it, and not all the corsets in Letchworth will support a drooping spirit. We are not talking about prosperity – the very phrase 'quality of life' was born at a time of apparently boundless prosperity, in order to suggest that there was something more. We are talking about happiness, contentment, peace of mind – or so I think. You will notice my hesitation there, for what I do not think is that we can or should be ever entirely happy and contented. Sunniclyffe Retirement Colony is a fraud because it pretends to be Utopia, and there is no Utopia, both because its inmates can never be perfectly good, and because the world around will never let it be at peace. Outside, the starving children wail, the tortured prisoners groan, the trees are poisoned, and the rivers run green with effluent.

Some of us, like the occupants of Sunniclyffe, can privatize the quality of life for a while. But faster and faster, the world catches up with them. I know people who retired comfortably in Kenya until independence chased them out. Then relaxed in Cyprus, until the Turks invaded. Then moved to Malta, until Mr Mintoff taxed them out. Now they are in the Isle of Man, fearful of a second coming by the Vikings. It is at least dawning on most of us that a privatized quality of life is too fragile to depend on. If we are going to measure it by quantities, we will have to share it, partly because material quantity makes other people jealous, and partly because, with very few exceptions, the production of material quantity is itself a community affair.

This is to state the position bereft of moral obligation. By which I mean that it is actually a sin to feather our own nest, regardless of our fellow men and women: by which, in turn, I mean that we are intended by God to love (that is, care for) one another. That is the true nature, the 'better self', for which we were designed. That is how we work best. But we are also endowed with the free will to think we know better and choose to do otherwise. We can, if we like, eliminate God from that equation and simply say that the quality of life is enhanced when we love one another. The trouble is, when we do eliminate him, we are liable to get some people saying that their rights to enhancement are greater than other people's rights. Under God, nobody has rights; only duties. There are, you will be shocked to hear, no such things as human rights: there are only human duties to 'that of God' in one another. But that is another lecture and will cost you another fee . . .

I will, however, give you this much for nothing: our duties stem directly from the fact of creation. We owe them, in love, to God for his loving act of creation. And it should come, logically, as no surprise that when we contemplate our duties to creation, they turn out to be the sensible thing to do; for they are in keeping with our designed nature. One of the crazy things about doing wrong is that it is usually nonsensical and illogical – contrary to our real interests. Unfortunately, that does not mean that moral questions are usually quite obvious, for all too often we are faced with several conflicting questions at once; that is why we call them 'problems'. The difficulty is: which question takes priority, which am I supposed to be answering?

I seem to have strayed into a third lecture. But it was worth hinting at in order to make the point that if there is some standard for the quality of life other than personal comfort, it does not have to be beyond the reach of reason. I am not saying that the whole of Christian ethics can be argued out by logic; there is more to it than that. But the Church has always recognized what is called natural morality: there are virtues like truth-telling, courage, and fidelity which are common to almost all cultures, and these are by and large virtues which make sense because society works better with them – they enhance the quality of life.

Even so, our material life goes better when we observe our duties towards creation, when we care for our fellow men and for the world around us, whether we see it as sensible and logical not to pour poison in rivers, or as returning the love of God not to vandalize his gifts. It is best, I think, to combine the two. The old Utilitarian maxim of pursuing the greatest good of the greatest number does not always meet the case, for what do we mean by 'good', or even 'happiness', and in how long a run? Still greater difficulties arise with the Utilitarian formula when you try to introduce values for plants and animals. Felling the rain-forests of Madagascar may bring great happiness to land-hungry peasants: lemurs and trees don't count. But even beyond that, does anybody care what it will mean for the soil and the climate? In this case, it seems illogical to buy short-term satisfaction at the cost of long-term disaster. But a more direct route is the conviction that it is a sin to violate what little is left of God's natural creation. And that surely applies to Tasmania as well. Some may say this religious approach is a romantic approach; but there are mighty truths in the romantic.

The examples of Madagascar and Tasmania are romantic in presenting the quality of life as the quality of all living things. It is romantic – and it is true – to say that the quality of my own life is interdependent with the life of the animals and trees, which is what ecology was originally about. But while I can afford to leave the trees up in my garden for the bullfinches to gorge themselves on my fruit buds, the peasant in Madagascar cannot. For him the quality of life is the quality of human life, or more personally, whether he and his family can stay alive at all.

It is not terribly helpful, at this point, to talk about giving him contraception, nor even sending him the Eurobutter mountain. I suspect he would not appreciate either; and in any case, I was thinking about him now, today. That is not to exclude the quality of human life tomorrow – his children's world; that is one way of interpreting 'the next world'. But at this halfway point, I wish to pick up a rather different meaning of my title's second part – 'This world – or the next?'

Now I do not actually know Madagascar. I have never been there but, as usual, I saw it on a television programme, and so was confident I could share it with the rest of you who have never been there either. But I do know India fairly well, and the quality of life there is certainly no better. In many parts it is worse; and I speak as one who witnessed the great Maharashtra drought of some ten years back.

Now, there are two things that always get me into trouble. One is my obstinate conviction that people are at least as important as animals – not the other way round. And the second is my observation that the poor of India have a blessed quality about their lives which we ought to envy. At first sight it appears to be nasty, brutish and short. Short it too often is, but it is lived with a sense of form and shape and colour, an acceptance of one's meaning and one's place in society and the universe, which is very rare in Christian Europe. It is all very well to say 'But no human being should be expected to put up with such an existence!' If India's poor did not put up with it and make the best of it – if their predominantly Hindu religion did not enable them to make some sense of it – there could be no alternative to a social explosion and national self-destruction. The quality of life to them has nothing to do with either string quartets or Jacuzzis. (Probably they would prefer the Jacuzzi, for Indian people have a great passion for washing and are mystified by how little Europeans seem to bath.)

Nor, of course, has the attitude of the Indian poor much to do with Christianity, since very few of them are Christians. I am not about to disparage the Christian faith for I know parts of India where its benefits are unquestionable; but it is not rooted in the culture, and the effects of conversion can be to cut the convert off from the society around him. One major difference between the Christian and the Hindu philosophy is in the rival doctrines of karma and redemption. The Hindu, believing in reincarnation, regards this life as the inevitable consequence of the merits or demerits gained in a previous existence. Promotion or demotion in the next life equally depends upon one's dedication to one's role in the present. Thus, it is flying in the face of fate to try and change oneself radically in the here-and-now.

The Christian, on the other hand, does not believe in reincarnation. It is nowhere to be found in the Scriptures or the teachings of the Church. The individual is emphatically called upon to change; but although his faith will be reflected in his good works, he cannot secure heaven in the next life by such works; but only by accepting God's grace.

These are two different approaches to the next world; but it will be seen that the Hindu view of the path towards it is a great deal more submissive and less demanding of initiative. The Christian view – especially when complicated by the doctrines of the fall, of original sin, and by the whole Christian obsession with sin – is a great deal more alarming, strenuous, full of doubts and fears. One is not engaged in an endless game of snakes and ladders (so to speak) but staking everything on the single throw of one life. The general view is that you die, appear before the Judgement Throne, and proceed immediately to heaven or hell, redeemed or damned for ever.

This is so drastic that, with the help of some detailed examination of Scripture, the Church has devised a more devious route. Since, surely, none of us can deserve immediate bliss, intermediate stages have been postulated like limbo (a sort of happy parking-lot for the innocent unredeemed) and purgatory (where the imperfect majority work off their forgivable sins). It will not be comfortable, but the faithful will acknowledge the justice of it and work their passage through. In some ways, it is not totally unlike the personal regrading implicit in reincarnation.

Now I agree totally with the much-travelled clergyman who said to me – in my *Priestland's Progress* series – 'If the humble Hindu on the banks of the Ganges cannot go to Heaven without becoming Church of England, Roman Catholic or United Reformed, then God is not the God I know or would want to know.' My own feelings upon observing India's poor – going about their business without ambition but with purpose, faith and a surprising amount of gaiety – was that if the Sermon on the Mount did not stand up there, if the poor were not blessed, if the meek did not inherit the earth, if the pure in heart were not to see God, then Christianity was a fraud. And I am as certain as I can be – because I trust the God I have met through Christ – that those poor will see God, most of them before I do.

That, I suppose, is what 'the next world' is about: seeing God – the beatific vision, at its highest. And what I propose to do now is to consider, first, what 'seeing God' can mean; second, what our experience in this world can have to do with it.

Seeing God! You cannot do it, certainly not now – or can you? Moses, we are told, spoke to him 'face to face, as a man speaketh unto his friend', and Jesus told his disciples that anyone who had seen him had seen the Father. And yet there is so much evidence that the visible God is a mere tip of the iceberg that – I think – if Jesus *was* God, yet there is still more to God than Jesus. It is amazingly generous of God to present himself to us in forms that our limited sense can grasp; but it is inconceivable that finite us could ever comprehend the infinite him. If the beatific vision is ever attained, it must surely swallow us all up – which may be the ultimate annihilation of the self that the East has in mind.

I think it is entirely right and proper that we do not know; if we knew too much about the next world, we would never get on with our duties in this one. And how do we know that there is a next one? That there is a God to be 'seen' – to any extent? The answer to both questions must be that we do *not* know – not in the sense that we know there is a cat in the garden – and that it is actually important that we should not. If we could prove, measurably, that there is a God, that there is a next world, the inevitability of it would destroy our freedom of will, our capacity for spiritual growth, our ability to love God and be loved by him. Instead of knowing in that sense (and I grant that some people would say there is a different sense) we believe, we trust, we have faith. I would say we do not have an unreasonable certainty, but a reasonable uncertainty.

A fully convinced Christian would say, I am sure, that our confidence in the next world is founded on the resurrection and testimony of Jesus. But if we are honest, many of us will confess that, deep down inside, we are not sure that his example will necessarily apply to us. And it was all rather a long time ago; and the details are a bit blurred.

What I find persuasive is this: if this world is not in some way a preparation for the next, then life is pretty absurd. In particular, it is absurd for human beings to have the spiritual equipment, the capacity to love each other and to love God that they do. And yet none of us (and least of all atheists, humanists and agnostics) live our lives as if they were absurd, and the spiritual parts of us perishable. I fancy we are programmed, designed by God, for immortality. We feel something urging us 'this way – this way – onwards – and beyond!' Perhaps I am getting romantic again. But if we are finite with this world, we are going about life the wrong way; so I do not believe that we are.

What we are chasing after all the time is nothing less than reality: what is this *really* about? What is its design, its purpose, its meaning? And that is God. Or rather, it is the God*head*, the God*hood*, and out of that Godhead proceeds his communication and caring for us, while up to it proceeds our communication and caring for him.

If so, then 'seeing God' – entering the next world – is going to be an experience of reality: if you like, 'seeing what it all means'. All? Well, perhaps not all at once; but at any rate, much more clearly than we do now. We shall, perhaps, understand why our life in this world has not been absurd.

The meaning – if Christianity has got anything right at all – will be something to do with love: with understanding ('seeing') God's love for us, and realizing (again 'seeing') how the way we have developed our capacity to love one another and to love creation affects our ability to love God and be loved by him.

So at this point I begin to build my bridge between this world and the next. I am sorry if the preliminary work of clearing the site and laying the foundations has been hard going, but I have to confess I am a stranger in this territory myself.

I have tried to suggest what 'seeing God' in the next world can mean; and my suggestion is that it means seeing the reality – the purposeful love – behind the experiences that have been heaped upon us in this one. It is an ancient and well-developed doctrine of the Church that such experiences mediate God to us: that God is revealed to us not just in Scripture and sacrament, but in nature (his creation) and in history. It is a somewhat less popular doctrine, but implicit in the incarnation, that God is revealed in humanity also, so that in loving one another (caring for one another) we are loving and caring for God. People are terrified of seeming to say 'Man is God', but my colleagues the Quakers have always insisted upon 'speaking to that of God in everyone' and we can point to that most awesome pronouncement of Christ in judgement: 'Inasmuch as you have done it unto one of the least of these my brothers, you have done it unto me.'

And again, 'I was hungry and you gave me nothing to eat; thirsty and you gave me nothing to drink; I was a stranger and you did not give me room; naked and you did not clothe me; in hospital and in prison and you failed to visit me.'

Now, whatever St Paul may say about justification by faith, Christ is here judging by works, and allows no excuse to those who say they failed to recognize him in their fellow men. He is saying 'What have you done with that world you have just left, for my brothers who were your brothers?' And let me remind you also of the Parable of the Talents: of the servants who were expected to invest and exploit the gifts entrusted to them, and not just bury them away in a safe place.

The gospels may not tell us much about the next world, but they do make it perfectly – damningly – clear that there is no real choice between the two. It is not 'this world *or* the next' – not political action *or* the life of prayer – it is both, it is 'this world *and* the next'. What is more, it is 'the next world *because of* this one': our next life will be a direct consequence of this one. The loving God is also a just God; he cannot be otherwise without violating his own nature. (Notice, by the way, how Christ in Judgement gives the accused the chance to plead guilty, to throw themselves on the mercy of the court – a chance which they obstinately reject by trying to argue excuses. This happens also in the Parable of the Talents. In the end, we condemn ourselves. We can choose to accept the God within us, or to pretend it is not there.)

So, if there is that bridge between this world and the next, if we want to see reality as love and not only justice, we dare not regard the two as being in isolation from one another. As I hinted a moment ago, I do not expect judgement to be quite so theatrical as St Matthew presents it – though he makes the point much better that way – but it is clear to me that our spiritual condition, like our physical shape, depends a great deal on how we exercise it here in this life. If we do not exercise our bodies, they become flabby, lethargic, incapable of responding when demands are made upon them. In the same way, if we do not use our spiritual faculties regularly, we shall eventually become incapable of competing in the spiritual world, in this world and the next. We all have those faculties, though our talents lie in different directions: some are direct, intuitive and uncomplicated, others elaborate and argumentative. The important thing is to develop the talents that we have by using them; and if we care at all about our chances in the next world, if we want to 'see God' – to grasp the reality – we must exercise them here and now.

Now, it is possible to engage in detached 'spiritual exercises' – there are such things – but it seems to me there is a danger of their becoming purely self-indulgent, or objects of worship for their own sake. Jesus was highly critical of people who thought it was enough simply to go through the motions of spiritual exercise. Even his sacramental gestures – I am thinking of Baptism and the Eucharist in particular – took place not in temples, but in the working world: he does not seem to have been much of a ritualist, or a believer in vain repetition. His view of exercising the spirit was to do what was set before him – in his case, to heal, to counsel, teach and encounter his neighbour; to love and to care for his Father's creation, into which he looked for the signs of the kingdom. And I think that is the sort of spiritual exercise to which we are all called.

It is quite central to both Christianity and Judaism to recognize that humanity's relationship with God is not a magical one. God is not 'up there' waiting to be manipulated by the right spells, rituals and sacrifices. He is already 'down here' in all sorts of forms presenting himself to us, eager for us to pick up the signals of his love and respond to them. This response – this two-way communication – is the essence of spiritual activity. God begins the exchange with the message of his love: we recognize it, appreciate it, realize it and return it – thus completing the circuit without which love is incomplete and frustrated. God actually depends upon our co-operation to make his love active and effective: he needs humanity if he is to *work*.

So we have to do two things in this world: we have to look deep into it – experience it, feel it, contemplate it – for the signals of God, his loving will; and then we have to work with (not against) those signals to bring it about.

Neither of these stages is easy for most of us, although I know some blest people to whom it is second (or rather, first) nature. It is hard enough to work with God's will when the systems of the world are pursuing their relentless logic in other directions. But going deep – learning to look into the world for its real meanings – is something we constantly skip; it is an awful lot of bother, we 'get things done' on the surface, where the sparkle is, and we move along much faster. But the trouble is, much of what we achieve is trivial or destructive, and when the reckoning comes, we find we have got nowhere. A great spirit of the Russian Orthodox Church, Metropolitan Anthony of Sourozh, once told me that sin was 'the refusal to go deep, where God is, and where all human beings are united in him'. What so many of us need is the capacity to calm ourselves, to stop floundering in a panic, so that we can sink into the deep and meet the God in the world around us and in each other. I would make a plea for less uproar, less busy-ness, even less liturgy in church and certainly less Muzak. But it is surprising how deep even a few seconds of calm – in a street, on a train, in the kitchen – will go. And that is what prayer really is.

If the quality of life means caring for this world and the people in it, and not merely hanging pretty ornaments on it to hide the deep-down neglect, then it will stand us in good stead in the next world also. I hope I have not disappointed you in failing to discuss the various practical things we might do to improve our care of it – banning pop music, limiting television to four hours a day, prescribing pets on the National Health Service, and compulsory replacement of all Dutch elm disease victims are just a few ideas – but the fact is, I am not a very practical person.

Which, of course, worries me; because, from what I have been saying, it appears that only those who have exercised the spirit in practical ways in this world are going to be in good shape for the next. I am indebted to Spike Milligan for the story about W. C. Fields, who, on his death-bed, surprised everyone by sending for a priest. The priest arrived to find Mr Fields thumbing thoughtfully through a Bible. 'What are you looking for?' asked the priest.

'Loopholes . . .' answered Fields.

I do hope there are some.

The John Armitage Memorial Lecture, delivered at Letchworth Settlement on 4 February 1983.

6

For all the saints

The subject of saints may seem an odd one for a Quaker: very unreformed, very Catholic, rather idolatrous. But I regard myself as an ecumenical Quaker – as a member of a lay society within the greater Church of God – and while I prefer to keep doctrines out of my own worship, I can understand why others need them. I see them as useful tools to work with, and it is in this spirit that I approach the subject of saints.

Let me outline my thesis. I agree that the saints have, in their time, been exploited and overgrown with mumbo-jumbo. But I think we do wrong to dismiss them as mere mediaeval superstition. They were, and still are, the most vital and unifying expression of faith available to us all – because they are the most like ourselves, the most human. That is their great advantage. The saints are not (on the whole) theologians; they do not talk a lot. It is in their simple *being* as servants to God and his world, that they show forth our common humanity at its best; and that *being* is undogmatic, it is ecumenical, and it is even thoroughly Quaker. The Society of Friends owes its foundation to its saints; and like every congregation that has any spiritual life today, it owes its continuance to the modest, everyday saints who are still among us, and still among you. That is my theme.

Incidentally, I should like to say at once that sainthood is above sex; though, the Church having been what it has been – sexist, if you will – male saints are still in the majority. But if, in generalizing, I refer to a saint as 'he', it is not in the least because I question the holiness of women. If anything, I think they are holier than men – if I may say so without being thought patronizing.

How did the saintly system ever get started? The early Church believed that the Lord himself would be returning shortly to make his own choice between the sheep and the goats. But the fact is, he did *not* return, and his followers were sorely persecuted. Miraculously, their faith survived, though many of the faithful perished; and it seemed perfectly reasonable for those who had not known the Lord personally to address their prayers to him 'in care of' the martyrs who must now be reaping their reward.

Now to a good Protestant, this is shocking: we all agree we need no intermediary with God – which is certainly what I myself believe. But for us, the world of the departed spirits is a good deal less familiar than it was for the early Christians; and can any of us honestly say that our conversations with God are as intimate and reassuring as a petition to someone we had actually known as a living person? What else would the martyrs be doing but interceding for members of their community on earth? It follows from Christ's own death and resurrection, through the Christian belief that death is not the end but a triumphant beginning, that the martyr has conquered, is free, has the very ear of the Lord.

But what about those relics, those gruesome remains upon earth? Oddly enough, the cult of the saints was not something the early Church borrowed from the pagans. Pagan Romans were quite as shocked by it as we are, for they thought the dead were ill-omened and polluting. I think the Christian cult of holy bones was basically a celebration of the world turned upside down. Those who to the pagan were criminals were to the Christian heroes. What seemed like a shameful defeat was a glorious triumph. What looked like disgusting carrion was priceless treasure. And where that treasure was, in tomb or shrine, there the martyred saint still kept a foot upon earth and an ear to the ground, and where his bones were was where you went to get in touch with him.

This was the case during the first two or three centuries of the Christian faith, when martyrs were a living and dying reality. They were recognized as such by the people, and the Church was not well enough organized as a hierarchy to assert much control. But when the Church became the official state religion, there were good reasons for taking the saints in hand at last. One was, quite simply, to stop the devaluation of sainthood. They were multiplying absurdly, not least because local bishops were extremely keen to appropriate to themselves the influence and income that holy relics could bring, notably from pilgrims.

But with fewer opportunities for martyrdom, it began to be argued that holy living might be as valuable to God as holy dying, especially when one had lived a life of austerity and sacrifice. Before long, the names of the saints were being woven into the fabric of the Mass and their pictures were being used to beautify the churches. People liked the idea of a local saint, who would understand their accent and their circumstances, or of a saint who specialized in their complaint or occupation. It is fashionable nowadays to say 'Your God is too small'; but to many simple people the mysterious notion of the Trinity or of Christ the Judge of all was just too big.

Of course, there was concern among theologians about overstepping the line to idolatry and polytheism. But Church and people wanted their saints, and it was ingeniously argued that there was a clear distinction between the 'whrship' that was owed only to God, and 'respect' and 'veneration' for the saints. The latter were not 'little gods', they were merely invisible servants of God who would deliver our prayers to him or, like attorneys at court, argue our case for us.

Following the age of martyrs, many saints were missionaries, and founders of churches; and most precious of all was to have the saint's tomb at the heart of the church, implying that even in death the saint remained the protector of his flock. Where a whole saint was not available, a bit or a chip of a saint might do. (This practice, incidentally, was not exclusively Christian; one finds it in Buddhism also, and like Christian relics, Buddhist relics are often endowed with powers of healing. There is, in fact, scriptural justification for this, for we are told that the bones of Elisha raised a man from the dead, and that folk were healed by handkerchiefs which had been pressed to the body of St Paul.)

I am certainly not going to defend the mediaeval traffic in relics, however. For some reason, while the Eastern Churches went in for ikons, the West went in for relics, of which the crusades provided an inexhaustible supply – including enough splinters of the True Cross to reconstruct Noah's Ark (there were bits of that, too, of course), our Lord's swaddling-clothes, our Lady's girdle, bread from the feeding of the five thousand, and sweat from our

Saviour's brow. The buying and selling of relics was eventually made illegal under canon law. But long before that, people – including bishops and kings – had resorted to grabbing what they fancied. King Canute was a notorious body-snatcher, and personally assisted in raiding St Paul's Cathedral for the body of St Alphege and in digging up St Mildred for his collection at Canterbury.

One of the saddest cases of dismemberment befell that lovely sixteenth-century Spanish nun, St Teresa of Avila. Nine months after her death, a church official had her dug up and, after admiring the firmness of her uncorrupt flesh, cut off her left hand, keeping the little finger as his personal charm. Three years later, appetite whetted, he exhumed the saint again and carried off the body, leaving the convent where she had lain with one arm as a consolation prize. Four more times, Teresa was resurrected and mutilated. The right foot, the left eye, part of the jaw, the heart, ribs and sundry portions of flesh were dispersed as far afield as Rome, Brussels and Mexico. When the Spanish dictator, General Franco, died he had at his bedside – as he had for forty years – a jewelled reliquary containing St Teresa's left hand. Alas, even today, people will not let the saints rest in peace. The remains of the Saxon King, Edward the Martyr, have quite recently become 'bones of contention' before the courts, with the Russian Orthodox Church – of all inappropriate denominations – trying to gain possession of them.

One could go on with such horror stories for hours, and the longer one does the more obvious it becomes that is the Church and its people – not the saints themselves – who are to blame.

These excesses were, of course, part of the origins of Protestantism, and most of us (I imagine) would still say Amen to Number 22 of the Thirty-nine Articles, denouncing what it calls 'the Romish Doctrine concerning . . . Images . . . Reliques, and also invocation of saints, . . . a fond thing vainly invented . . . but rather repugnant to the Word of God'. Even so, Anglican churches have, in their usual ambiguous way, kept the saints in their prayer-books and have toyed, from time to time, with the idea of making saints of their own. The Church of England, in its new Service Book, has a list of 'Lesser Festivals and Commemorations' which include such figures as the poet George Herbert, John and Charles Wesley, John Bunyan and Josephine Butler.

At one time George Fox, the founder of the Quakers, was a candidate for that list; and personally, I am rather glad he failed to make it: it would never do for Quakers to have to *venerate* their founder or address their prayers through him. He is disqualified, I think, by some rather negative qualities in his character, for he was intolerant and unpleasantly vindictive; but when it comes to miracles, he did have something like 150 healings to his credit, including two or three claimed cases of raising from the dead.

But before we move on to the modern saint, I feel we should note two or three classic symptoms of saintliness which are not generally recognized but which are nevertheless quite frequent. The first, which I have already mentioned in the case of St Teresa, is the incorruption of the body after death, with the flesh remaining pliable and (as is often mentioned) fragrant. St Cuthbert, who died in 687 and was carted around Scotland and England for the next three hundred years, before coming to rest at Durham, was found to be presentable in 1104, On the other hand, nobody bothers to dig up a control group of notorious sinners; and the Eastern Orthodox Churches take the diametrically opposed view that the refusal of a body to corrupt is a sure sign of heresy, so that Rome's saint may be Constantinople's heretic.

Nevertheless, it does seem to be a characteristic of saints to smell sweet. Furthermore, almost without exception, animals feel at ease with them – St Francis of Assisi is the extreme example, and there was the Irish St Kevin, in whose hands a blackbird hatched her egg – and I find it really is a quality of people whom I identify as saints, that the animal kingdom relaxes in their presence, knowing it has nothing to fear and that it is at a point of harmony in the universe.

A very few saints had the power of levitation or instant travel through space: Teresa was certainly one of them – the evidence is all the more convincing because she fought against it, sometimes hanging onto furniture to stop herself rising into the air. But I cannot help feeling it a rather pointless accomplishment, like so many demonstrations of the occult. I prefer to emphasize one very common quality of saints, both past and present; that they create around themselves an atmosphere in which it is easier to be good. It is not that they intimidate us or make us feel guilty – quite the contrary: it is that their openness and simplicity puts us at ease and calls forth the natural goodness in us. Unexpectedly, saints are relaxing. They pose no threat to us, they demand no formalities nor feigning, they make goodness seem natural. We sense very much what the animals sense.

I suppose the Reformation really marks the borderline between the old-fashioned saint and the new. Under attack, the Roman Church begins to create saints on the grounds of their devotion to doctrine: they are less justified now by their works than by their faith. And on the Protestant side, we find much the same deviation – the development of the lay saint who is not so much holy as 'saved', and he is saved by faith or, more debatable still, by predestination. To do them justice, the Presbyterians did not claim to be certain about who was elect to salvation and who was damned; but the so-called Independents demanded visible signs of regeneration and proofs of sanctity. This was bound to involve works, but those works were to arise only from the great conversion of faith, and were the only reliable signs of it. And the road to such conversion was less likely to be through mystical or sacramental experience than through listening to sermons which expounded the true Protestant doctrine.

Now I would maintain that another essential characteristic of the saint is that he or she is a servant, which surely is the fundamental message of St Francis. But the Puritan saint, obsessed with the importance of correct faith, turned selfishly inward. He must not gamble, drink, swear or break the Sabbath; all of which might make him look virtuous and saved, but was of little service to others. It was precisely the sort of Pharisaism that Jesus condemned. Where were the expressions of love? Congregations of saints like these tended to be more concerned with the punishment of sin; and it was precisely this 'roaring up for sin' that nauseated George Fox.

I actually think that Fox was a recovered depressive, who broke through to an overwhelming sense of forgiveness. For he began to make claims such as no Catholic saint ever dared make: that he was 'a man without sin', that he was 'come up through the flaming sword into the paradise of God, and was in that same state wherein Adam was before he fell'. 'Christ', he said, 'hath taken away my sins.' Not surprisingly, he was jailed for saying so – again and again.

This idea that man might actually achieve perfection through Christ is an ancient and persistent heresy – Wesley toyed with it, too – and quite apart from the doctrine of original sin, I think it is just plain contrary to human experience. However, Fox simmered down a bit as he grew older, and he did display many of the other qualities of a saint: the simplicity and the service (as a healer, a missionary, and a tireless defender of the persecuted and imprisoned). But above all – in spite of what I have said about his unattractive qualities – he was deeply loved and was, quite simply, a man in whose presence people found it easier to be good.

I have argued that the true saint affects the world through his or her life and personality, rather than through words, and I am sure this is true of Fox. Not that he was not a wordy man; he poured out a torrent of pamphlets and epistles, most of which are heavy going to us. But that is not really what Quakers owe to him today. What they owe is a few basic insights into humanity's relations with God: the use of silence, the simplicity, the openness and peacefulness and courage and – not least – Fox's genius as an organizer. And this kind of thing is true of all the great figures of Nonconformist religion: not the tracts they wrote, but the tradition they handed down by the force of their example.

You will remember that the great thing about the very earliest of the martyr-saints was that they were believed to have direct access to the Lord. This was the heart of Fox's message also: that we can all have such access, that we can all be saints in the measure of the light given us. And after Fox came a torrent of modest everyday saints of all denominations. What mattered was less what they had to say than what they were: the way they confronted the powerful, acted out their convictions and endured their persecutions. It is not their theology that speaks to us today so much as their stories. And story – human character reacting with the world – can still embody truth even when it is polished into myth. For that is what very often happened with the saints of old, and I hope I do not give too much offence when I venture to say it happens often in the Bible. Nobody was there taking down every detail in a notebook, and the truth that is expressed is not necessarily the literal truth but the essential truth – just as a poem can be profoundly true, though literally absurd. Let us think of the lives of the saints, then, as holy poems rather than history.

But today, and for some time past, people actually have been there with notebooks and our knowledge of people and events is much more literal. Thanks to science, perhaps we have become too literal for our own good as spontaneous human beings. We find it hard to allow anyone the perfection of the saints of old, for we are always sniffing suspiciously for the rancid small of hypocrisy – an unlovely trait in us, for I think the one real hypocrisy is to denounce it in others. As a matter of fact, I doubt whether many of the classic saints were much better than the saints we know today; they were just less jealously reported, and by fewer reporters. The stories that have come down to us have been brushed and combed, but their essential truths are not therefore misleading. We may think that the age of saints is past, not only because there are no more miracles (though that is questionable) but because our contemporary candidates cannot be retouched and varnished in the way that saints used to be. We are too envious, too cynical, too ready to headline the negative – too disillusioned to let the positive shine forth.

But, as I say, saints are the very best way of showing what faith can do; and at a time when people are rightly suspicious of the claims of doctrine it is tempting to say 'We need more faith, so let us identify more saints'. All the equipment of public relations and the mass media are at our disposal, and some religious bodies are all too well aware of this. The world has seldom been so aware who its contemporary saints are: Mother Teresa of Calcutta, obviously; and there are airborne saints like John Paul II and Dr Billy Graham; martyr saints like Archbishop Luwum of Uganda, Archbishop Romero of El Salvador and Dr Martin Luther King. Bishop Desmond Tutu of Johannesburg is another candidate in my opinion. At the opposite end of the scale are such self-promoted candidates as Mr Sun Myung Moon, Mr L. Ron Hubbard and a gaggle of dubious gurus. We see here the dangers of modern saint-making, and perhaps we in the Reformed tradition can thank ourselves for two things: that we have no possible procedure for canonizing anyone, and that the classical saints have made us expect something in the way of magic that we cannot have anyway.

Let me mention two fairly recent examples of people who undoubtedly deserve to be ranked as saints, and yet seem too ordinary, too workaday for the title.

I think first of William Carey, the self-educated Baptist cobbler from Northamptonshire, who went out to India early in the last century at a time when the policy of the East India Company was to ban missionaries, on the grounds that they would spread discontent among the poor and encourage uppitiness among the natives in general. Carey first spent six years growing indigo to raise funds, while at the same time studying the local languages. Then he set up in a tiny Danish colony, where the gospel was not forbidden, and brought in a team of helpers. Not only did they create a Christian college (which still survives), but as an offshoot of their work as translators and printers of the Bible they also founded the newspaper and publishing industries in India. They lived together in a commune, and they died like flies, and in their congregations they made the first breach in the caste system. Together they were the apostles of Bengal.

I think next of two Quaker saints: James Backhouse and George Washington Walker, who in the 1830s felt the call to go out to Australia, which in those days was being stocked as a prison colony, and where the Aboriginal inhabitants were being decimated. 'I was in prison and ye visited me' says the Lord to those whom he rewards with a place in heaven, and that is precisely what Backhouse and Walker did, as part of their religious duty. They also preached in the evangelical tradition, but as one observer remarked, 'Instead of preaching too much, they kept accounts and kept them carefully. With a view to practical results they were careful to note facts with draper-like precision.'

These facts, on conditions in the convict ships and in the colonies and among the Aborigines, they sent back to England as ammunition for reformers like Elizabeth Fry; and they reported so accurately and conscientiously that the authorities were compelled to accept their reports and eventually to act upon them. In a sense, they practised the best kind of journalism; but the interesting thing is that they managed to dig up the truth without making themselves unacceptable to authority, and whenever one reads about them in official correspondence, they are always referred to in tones of the highest esteem. One Governor's wife – Lady Denison of Tasmania – describes Walker as 'the very personification of a mild, benevolent and excellent Quaker . . . men of all denominations unite in speaking well of him . . . he is never mentioned without respect . . . and whatever good is to be done, he is sure to have a hand in it.' Could there be a better definition of a practical saint? And is that so different from the people you will find today, not only in aid and relief projects overseas (both Christian and secular) but here at home and at your very elbow?

Any Meeting or congregation that I know which has the Light of the Spirit in it owes that light to the presence in the midst of it of two or three everyday saints – maybe with a very small 's', but saints they are. And everyone knows who they are (except, I suspect, themselves). They are by no means necessarily elders or ministers, nor do they necessarily say very much. When they are absent, something intangible goes out of the congregation; and when they are present (even though silent) the congregation is capable of its best again. It is almost telepathic, and it is at its best where a congregation is truly a society of friends who know and love one another and are sensitive to one another's presence. In the presence of our friendly everyday saint, we find it easier to be good and to discover the goodness in ourselves. Such holiness – a modest holiness – is undogmatic, unaccusing, and for that reason truly ecumenical, for it is rooted in the common humanity of us all (which is the will of God, not of humanity).

And it is this humanity that convinces people. When I examine my conscience as to why I trust in God, I find that fundamentally it is because I trust others – my personal saints who themselves trust in God and whose lives show me their trust is reliable. Some of them are Quakers; some Protestant, some Catholic, some Orthodox, some Jews; and some have been dead a long time. A few – like Francis of Assisi – are saints with a big 'S', through whom I can see the light of the Spirit shining as through a stained-glass window. In some ways, saints are better dead – for they are less likely to do things that will disillusion you.

But, on the other hand, there is nothing you can do for a saint who is dead. One advantage of your modest local saint is that you can not only respond to her love and openness, but return it. And this is my last word: I know you must have such folk in your church, or it would not be here. I urge you, then, to recognize, respect and care for your saints, and they – not I – will show you the Light.

This is a slightly abridged version of a talk given at Wilmslow United Reformed Church on 14 October 1984.

God and Man

7

Vices and virtues

During occasional fits of revulsion from the age we live in, I sometimes wish I were a mediaeval man. In a sense, I already am: a man of middle age, half way between the barbarism of youth and the supposed equanimity of old age. But what I really like about the mediaeval approach is its tidy passion for classifying things – in which it rather resembles the Hindu. As in the Kama Sutra (a work whose author, by the way, assures us it is pure theory unsullied by any practical experience), everything in mediaeval knowledge has a name, a place in the hierarchy, an exact position on some parchment chart. Logic inspired by theology governed all things. Scientific observation had barely arrived to confuse the scholars with facts.

The trouble is today that science keeps altering the facts, so there is no stability in the theories. Just as we think we understand something, it changes its shape, melts into something else, turns out to be something quite different. And this is worst of all in the field of human behaviour, where for a while X is recognized as a social response or an economic phenomenon, then turns into a psychological fantasy, but ends up being treated as a chemical imbalance. Almost any of these approaches can be made to make sense for a time, which is what we really hanker after: a pattern, an explanation, an assurance that in man we have something that makes sense, and not just a packet of chaos.

Good and bad, white and black, God and the devil, virtue and vice – that is how we would *like* to sort things out. Basically, Either/Or; for Both/And implies contradictions and complications which are too unsettling. There must (we tell ourselves) be a right answer and a wrong one. We imagine ourselves at a parting of the ways: turn left for misery and damnation, or right for happiness and life eternal. But in our hearts we have always known that it is not so simple. A great deal of moral theology is concerned with explaining – or trying to explain away – why. And very difficult it is, because if God is good (and only the most recondite heresies have suggested otherwise), then surely he cannot have made it well-nigh impossible for us to follow his chosen way. And yet, what he is thought to want seems to conflict so often with the sort of life we find ourselves living. We search for a guide to the paths of righteousness.

One of the oldest and most familiar catalogues of virtue is the Ten Commandments. There are at least three versions of these to be found in the Old Testament, but to simplify, they come down to these:

Only One God; no experimenting with other gods; no light use of the name of the one God; observe his holy day; honour your parents; do not murder; do not commit adultery; do not steal; do not lie; do not hanker after other people's property.

(You will notice that loving your neighbour as yourself is not in the classic list, though it is indeed to be found in the expansion of it in Leviticus, chapter 19; it was not an invention of Jesus. It is Jewish in origin and not uniquely Christian.)

Now it seems to me that the Ten Commandments amount to something much less abstract and metaphysical than a summary of virtue: they are the rules and regulations of a club, in this case a tribe. In fact they are the conditions of a contract between Jehovah and the Children of Israel, the particular price Jehovah demanded in exchange for protecting and favouring them. There is no question in the early books of the Old Testament but that there are other gods: it is just that Jehovah is getting the exclusive rights to Israel, cutting the other gods out. The last six commandments lay down the club rules for social and economic activity, including family discipline and property rights. This is not exactly what I would call virtue – though there is a lot to be said for continuing to observe the Ten Commandments.

I know a man, a don at Cambridge, who tries very hard to observe them as practical rules of everyday life. He tells me that the commandment he most values is the one on Sabbath observance: it is the only way he can resist the modern middle-class compulsion to work seven days a week, and he reckons it will add years to his life. The hardest one, he tells me, is the one against bearing false witness, because he takes that as forbidding Common Room gossip.

Now as we know, one of the reasons for the development of Christianity was that a highly legalistic and mechanical application of the covenant between Israel and Jehovah simply ceased to satisfy; for one thing, it did not secure the safety of Israel; for another, it was obvious that meticulous observance of the rules did not necessarily produce virtuous people, nor did it make them feel any closer to or more reconciled with God, who remained a capricious, unreasonable and frankly unlovable person. Yet there were people who knew him to be otherwise, of whom Jesus was one.

But I propose to keep his view of the matter until later. For the present I shall take a leap of several centuries into the sixth century AD, when St Gregory the Great drew up his list of the seven deadly sins – deadly not just because each one was morally grave in itself, but because it was infectious and gave rise to others.

Gregory's list has echoes of the Commandments, but it is now much less earthy. No longer have we anything relating to the 'one God' rules (which had already been nailed down in the creeds), while the laws about family and property had been taken care of by civil law. What we have now, much influenced by Greek philosophy, is a series of abstract anti-virtues. They are:

Pride, always the first and gravest; covetousness, lust and envy, all of which have links with the Commandments; gluttony, which is not at all Mosaic; anger and sloth, which are far from implicit in the Commandments.

I describe these as abstract. But Middle Eastern and North European peoples have never cared much for abstractions: their tribal religions have always asserted the existence of demons and devils who tempted and even possessed men from the outside. This is convenient from two points of view: the artistic (since it is much more satisfactory to paint or describe a real and external demon), and the psychological: 'I wanted to be good, but the devil tempted me . . .'.

The finest parade of the seven deadly sins is to be found in that least-read classic of English literature, Spenser's *Faerie Queene*, of which very few have ever got beyond the first stanza. It was archaic when Spenser wrote it, unreadable from the start, with all those ekes and eftsoones and allegories within allegories within allegories. But nobody has ever had the heart to tell poor

Spenser his epic was a white elephant. There are six books of twelve cantos each, each canto having about fifty stanzas, and each stanza having nine lines – making more than 32,000 lines in all, which is a very wordy elephant.

However, in Canto Four of Book One the False Duessa rides forth in her coach, conducted by her steward Vanity (which of course is sin number one, that is, Pride) and drawn by six beasts upon which are seated her 'six sage counsellors'.

The first was 'Sluggish Idleness' (that is, Sloth) 'the nurse of sin'. He is dressed like a monk, to show what Spenser thought of the Old Church, and he takes no exercise.

By his side is Gluttony, grossly fat, 'And in his hand did beare a bouzing can' (for gluttony is always taken as including drunkenness). He is diseased, he vomits detestably, and is oblivious of the starving poor.

'And next to him rode lustful Lechery' – a vile, goatish creature who (sighs Spenser) is quite irresistible to the ladies, for (he adds) 'Who does know the bent of women's fantasy?' (I am afraid Spenser was a male chauvinist.)

Fourth in the troop rides 'Greedy Avarice' – that is, Covetousness – and the interesting thing about him (a very mediaeval concern) is that for all the gold he carries with him, he is a miser. He spends nothing on himself, so that a Devil's Advocate might plead that he is the very model of self-denial. One interesting consequence of his love of money for its own sake is that he is totally amoral, like a successful investment banker. He lends money on interest, 'And right and wrong in equall ballaunce waide', says Spenser.

Next we have Envy, who delights in disaster.

> So every good to bad he doth abuse:
> And eke the verse of famous Poet's witt
> He does backbite, and spightfull poison spues
> From leprous mouth on all.

(I get the impression that Spenser was having trouble with the critics.)

And beside Envy there rode 'fierce revenging Wrath' – Anger, that is. Wrath, we are told, is uncontrollable and splashed with blood. Today we might associate him with violence.

So there they are, the paradigms of the mediaeval seven

deadly sins, and people still make films and plays and ballets about them. Turn them over (as it were) and you find on the backs of them Christian virtues: for pride, humility; for covetousness, poverty; for lust, chastity; for envy, sympathy; for gluttony, abstinence; for anger, love; and for sloth, the Protestant work ethic – plus healthy outdoor exercise. Incidentally, C. S. Lewis could never understand why physical exercise was considered to be an antidote to vice: no one, he pointed out, was more physically exercised than soldiers, and yet soldiers were notoriously lustful.

Oddly enough, the traditional seven virtues of the Church are not, as one might have expected, the reverse of the seven deadly sins. The virtues were chosen on a different basis: the four cardinal virtues of the ancient world – classical Greek virtues, namely prudence, temperance, fortitude and justice – together with faith, hope and charity. The four classics go back to Plato and Aristotle; and while none of them could be called anti-Christian, they are the sort of natural good qualities you might expect of any pagan society. Prudence, I suppose, might rule out wrath; temperance should control gluttony and lust (on the principle of 'Nothing in Excess'); fortitude would not come naturally to the slothful; and justice should preclude covetousness and envy. But I would suggest that there is something fundamentally unsatisfactory about trying to break down vices or virtues into neatly fitting components of human nature.

I have to say that I do not even find faith, hope and charity altogether satisfactory as a summary of the Christian foundations. Faith is all very well in so far as it means trust in God, in his goodness, his fatherhood and his purpose for us all; but it has a way of sliding into statements like 'you must believe in the Athanasian Creed, the Thirty-nine Articles and the infallibility of Scripture' – which I for one do not, although I challenge anyone to take away my claim to be Christian.

Hope can be most unsatisfactory: not, indeed, if it means waiting patiently upon God; but it can also imply a certain hopelessness – an inferior grade of uncertain faith. And as for charity: of course it is love – the most important of all Christian qualities and the very principle of God – but it is a simple word for a complex and difficult concept. The Greeks, we know, had three or four different words representing sexual love, friendship, fellowship and spiritual love; we, clumsily, use the same word for all. But even the Greek terms are not watertight: they overlap and leak into each other. I do not think the Church was acting solely from prudery when it treated sexual love as if it were a dangerous competitor. When two people love each other, it is a genuine peak experience, having more in common with religious experience than many people like to admit. And when somebody has undergone a religious conversion, they are very like somebody who has fallen in love. I am quite sure, myself, that the need to give love (even more than to receive it) is vital to the health and depth of the human soul. But, by itself, love indeed is blind. It needs certain other qualities to become practical: for example, a certain toughness.

What I wish to suggest is that the classical lists of virtues and vices no longer speak to our condition today; which is hardly surprising, since we are not Children of Israel, nor are we mediaeval man. Although I am not suggesting that there are no moral standards, I believe that written formulations of them can go out of date, and that the Holy Spirit itself did not fall silent on the matter once the last full stop had been put to the Book of Revelation. If it had, we should have to agree that God is dead.

I do not expect that I shall be able to convince some of you that I am not being blasphemous, when I take issue – at a certain level – with the Ten Commandments. But I have to say that those of us who are believers at all need no instruction from Mount Sinai to be sure that there is one God only, that we should not kill, steal or lie and so forth; indeed, one does not even have to be a believer to accept the tail end of the Decalogue – it makes good sense socially and has become part of our culture. But, you may say, people still disobey it; it needs to be asserted. Maybe so, but it does not make a religion; there is surely more to the Christian way of life than this. And then, of course, we remind ourselves that Christianity combines Old and New Testaments, and that the message of Christ was that obeying the Law of Moses is not enough for salvation: overcoming sin requires more than ritual observance. What I am groping towards is a wholeness – a final break with the idea that there are certain good points which we must score, certain bad points which we must avoid, in order to achieve redemption.

I have suggested that the old categories were formed in response to the demands of their age. The central driving force behind the Ten Commandments was the need to forge a strong, disciplined nation out of the Children of Israel: one solid theology and an unshakeable family structure. The Middle Ages – if we take the reverse of the seven deadly sins as the governing standards – needed to keep people in their places through humility, needed to keep them working hard at their jobs, and needed to keep the lid on envy, lust and gluttony as a matter of law and order. Prudence, temperance, fortitude and justice (you will notice) are very much upper-class, public-school virtues, the virtues required of the born leader rather than the common people; just as faith, hope and charity are the virtues of the religious.

I could not pretend for one moment that Spenser's nasty troop are off the road altogether today, though there may have been a change or two in their pecking order. Let us re-examine them.

Pride (or vaingloriousness, as it is sometimes called): moral theologians have always considered it the deadliest of the lot because it amounts to extreme selfishness – putting oneself and one's interests before God or one's neighbour; at its worst, the abuse of power. But psychiatrists rightly insist that there is no more fatal neurosis than the complete rejection of self, that we cannot love our neighbour unless we love (that is, value) ourself. And there are those who say that our nation today is suffering from a severe lack of national pride – lack of pride in our job, our family, our community – a refusal to recognize the good in them.

Covetousness: certainly we are often too fond of material possessions. But I have to say that I find this more a sin of the middle-aged than of the young. My own children and their friends are a good deal more modest in their demands for comfort than I was at their age. In any case, can there never be an honest theology of affluence? It may be hard for a rich man to enter into the kingdom of heaven, but is it impossible?

Then lust – ah, luscious lust! I suppose there is plenty of that about, though I honestly do not think that when our Lord made his famous remark about adultery in the heart, he meant that we were never to look at a pretty girl with approval (what matters is the intention). And am I wrong, I wonder, in thinking that with all the visual substitutes and pharmaceutical precautions we have today, the expression of lust is actually less beastly than it used to be? Sado-masochistic pornography might be brought in evidence against me, but I suspect it is largely a surrogate for the real thing: Victorian London concealed much nastier things than modern Soho displays.

Envy, possibly, is much worse today than it was. There was little point in the mediaeval peasant envying his master, because he had no hope of catching up with him. Today at least he thinks he has, and there are all sorts of influences urging him on.

Gluttony: a lobbyist for the Third World would have little doubt that most of the Northern Hemisphere is gluttonous. But within this country, inequalities notwithstanding, it is hard to find the glaring contrasts between overnourished and undernourished that sickened Spenser. Drunkenness and alcoholism may perhaps be worse; but we do not find it necessary to prosecute overeaters the way we do overdrinkers.

Anger, again, may have got worse. Probably there was more mugging and knifing during the Middle Ages than there is today; but what I am thinking about, of course, is the arrival of terrorism. What makes it look more serious is the advance of weapons technology: today's angry man does not lash out with a billhook; he draws a gun or puts a bomb in a market-place.

And what about sloth? I dare say there are people who spin out their tea-breaks and do not give a fair day's work for a day's pay; but personally I am more concerned (along with my Cambridge friend) about the over-activity of modern life. There is not enough stillness and contemplation. There is too much pointless business. But we still have this ruling-class Protestant conviction that unless the workers are kept at their benches they will get up to mischief – riot in the streets, or indulge in lust and gluttony. Sloth has always sent a shiver up the Anglo-Saxon spine: we tell ourselves it is a Latin vice, even though maybe the Latins are really the more civilized.

Not only are the traditional deadly sins modified by conditions today; I suggest that in some respects our life actually makes them much harder to resist. Pride, for example: now I did propose that in some cases there was insufficient of it; but on the other hand there are influences urging it on: the whole competitive spirit at school, in sport, in business. Despite the United Nations and the European Community, the world is still at the mercy of the pride of nationalism. We are proud when we beat another country – and our politicians still exploit this.

Take covetousness: what else is advertising about? Why else

do our trade unions (including mine) fight to defend the living standards of their members, including the car, the packaged holiday and the deep freeze?

Take lust: what with tight-fitting jeans, underwear advertisements in the Underground and twitching thighs on television, how can one avoid a twinge of it? Faced with such provocation, it is a wonder there are not more bottoms pinched.

Or envy: knowing that this is the age of the expense account and the credit card, how shall we not envy the smart new car of the man next door, or the apparently effortless success of those famous people in the Sunday papers? Misleading, of course, because we may not realize that the man next door is crippled with debt and the famous personality is on the verge of a divorce and a nervous breakdown – but nonetheless, we envy. Some say it is the basis of our party political system.

Gluttony, too, is hard to resist with all those colour advertisements. And once back home from the office, after battling first with your dear colleagues and then with the traffic, there's nothing nicer than a still anaesthetic Scotch and a mound of beef curry.

As for sloth: well, after five or six days like that, who can begrudge you a nice lie-in on Sunday morning? Our modern labour-saving devices are actually devices for making us do more labour than we were ever designed to cope with – including a day's worth of travel, quite apart from the work. Where (I wonder) does Sabbath observance merge into sloth?

So I will say it again: the sort of life we have staggered into makes it, in fact, far more difficult for us to resist the sort of vices that mediaeval man got very worked up about, but had relatively little chance to indulge in.

I have missed out one vice, on purpose, because my wife has asked me to tell you she has very strong feelings in favour of it: namely, anger. She feels that what with the frustration, provocation and *information* that comes beating down on us, it is very hard not to get angry. My wife says she never held with the mediaeval view anyway: she thinks it is entirely proper to get angry in a good cause, and that bottling up one's rage is both insincere and (in the long run) far more destructive than letting it rip. Most psychotherapists seem to agree with her – and did our Lord not permit himself righteous indignation?

So having demolished the old-fashioned vices and virtues,

or at least having reduced them to a confused mess, what are we left with?

It seems to me that our moral frameworks are in fact constructed from three directions: what is traditional, what is socially and economically necessary, and how each of us sees himself. What appear to be morally prescriptive statements (prescribing what you ought to do) are often conditional descriptive statements (describing what you would do if . . .). People who say 'You ought not to do that' often mean 'If you were me, you would not do that'. And their image of themselves may involve 'me' as a pacifist, 'me' as an animal-lover, 'me' as a Christian, and so forth.

Now I can only speak as 'me', and that happens to involve being a Quaker. Naturally I am influenced by the Quaker view of man, which (when it comes to sin) is a rather curious one.

George Fox, the founder of Quakerism, had the experience which he described as 'being taken up through the sword into the Paradise of God . . . to that state Adam was in before he fell'. And he emerged from this sublimely confident that he was liberated from sin. (Indeed, they kept throwing him in jail for saying so, and people came from miles around to inspect this unique exhibit, a man free from sin; while the clergy, as he put it, 'roared up for sin'.)

Ever since, Quakers have been oddly unconcerned about vices and sin, preferring to approach human nature from the end of original goodness, rather than original sin. It is heretical, of course, a partial truth like most heresies, but it appeals to us, and it is perhaps a valuable corrective to what has been called 'the sin-sodden liturgy of the Book of Common Prayer'.

I do not myself think that God is as worked up about sin as we are. He knows perfectly well (having designed us) that we are imperfect, that we will be constantly falling short of the mark. But he would much rather we picked ourselves up and got on with the business of loving one another than stay on the floor moaning about how sinful we are. Jesus himself had a most intriguing attitude towards sinners: he positively preferred them to the righteous. He found them better company, more frank, honest and open about themselves. At the top of his list of vices and hypocrisy, a very deadly form of pride. High up on his list of virtues was integrity, which means more than just honesty – it means a spontaneous wholeness, with nothing concealed, everything accepted: an openness to God, to life, to our fellow men and women. And such openness is only possible to people who trust in the fatherhood of God, who have absolute confidence (as St Francis de Sales puts it) that 'He will either shield you from suffering or give you unfailing strength to bear it'. And this I would call trust, rather than faith, not only because trust is a much warmer word, but because I do not think it has much to do with those Creeds or Articles of Scriptures that can so easily lead us away down doctrinal passages, away from the presence of God.

It is the Quaker belief that the Inward Light of God is present in all of us, if only we will let the mud settle and the light shine through; and that when we examine our problems in that light, it will show us what is right and what is wrong. We do not need a checklist of vices and virtues. What we need above all is the capacity for stillness.

I have, I suppose, been playing something of a game with you in this lecture: having set up the seven deadly sins and the seven virtues only to knock them down. So perhaps the least I owe you is to suggest some replacements for them. Who would be pulling Duessa's coach if we passed it on the road today? And what would the opposing team, the virtues, be?

Well, I have suggested **trust** – trust in God – as the principal white horse. So it follows that **mistrust** of him is the opposite – though let me add speedily that honest doubt, in the sense of seeking but not yet having found, is to be respected.

The way to trust, I am convinced, lies through **stillness**. And who today would question me when I put **noisiness** among the ungodly qualities?

Nobody, I think, would deny **violence** its place in the devil's team; or **non-violence** among the horses of the Lord.

Love, of course, pulls in harness with it – and pulling in the opposite direction, **hatred**. Hatred, I think, is very close to envy, so I need not include that.

I must say I have a good deal of sympathy for poor old – often misunderstood – lust. I shall get myself into trouble here if I do not have something like lust on one side, because if I do not I can hardly have chastity on the other. But do I really want chastity? I am not against it, if you like that sort of thing – but I would not want it to be confused with compulsory celibacy or the Puritan view of sex. If we must have a sexual virtue (and I think we should) then I choose **fidelity** – with **infidelity** in the opposing team.

Which brings me up to five-a-side. **Integrity** I have already tipped, for it encompasses openness, honesty, sincerity, spontaneity, and I wish I could make it include joyfulness as well. At any rate, it puts **dishonesty** (or hypocrisy, if you like) among the villains.

For my last virtue, I would like to find something to oppose the modern equivalents of gluttony – not just greedy eating and drinking, but greed for material possessions, and greedy squandering of the earth's resources. This would be the ecological, conservationist virtue: small is beautiful and 'Spare that Tree'. **Frugality** or restraint might do – moderation, even – confronting **wastefulness.**

Nothing but tradition obliges me to stop. I have half a mind to squeeze in **cruelty** and **selfishness** as vices – **generosity** and **modesty** as virtues; but I think they may be relatives of one or another that I have named already. So I will rehearse them again:

My seven modern deadly sins are:

Noisiness: Violence: Hatred: Infidelity: Dishonesty: Mistrust in God's Goodness: Wastefulness.

And my seven modern virtues:

Trust in God's Goodness: Stillness: Non-violence: Fidelity: Integrity: Love: Restraint.

Maybe, though it is a bit late in the day to say this, it is rather unQuaker to brandish the word virtue at all. In so far as these are identifiable qualities, are they not what we should assume to be characteristic of a normal human being, not something to be picked out and praised like good boys in a naughty class? And may it not be equally unQuaker to 'roar up for sin' by naming vices? Might we not prefer the more modest word 'faults'? Ah, that way lies a pitched battle! I can hear the Calvinists crying: 'Typical wishy-washy do-good Quakerism! Sins are sins – not mere faults. Next thing you'll be describing sin as some kind of computer malfunction.' (Actually, that is an interesting idea – and I really prefer the word faults.)

And so I arrive at the whole purpose of this exercise, which is to demolish itself – to explode the myth that vices are demons we can exorcize, and the virtues angels that we can woo – that either of them are external to ourselves. We cannot wholly remove any of them: they fall into a wholeness – one the better side of us, the other the worse. The important thing is to recognize that none of us is wholly on the one side or the other. Each of us entertains both. They are parts of the whole you, the whole me, and only when we accept that can we appreciate the real meaning of the devastating statement 'Your sins are forgiven'.

Lecture given before students of Manchester Polytechnic on 25 June 1980.

8

Matrimony – holy and not so holy

I am one of nature's pessimists, so I have the gloomy conviction that many of you will leave here convinced that I have said marriage has no connection with religion and that it does not matter much whether couples are wedded, bedded or shredded. If fact, this is the opposite of what I believe. I do believe in an old-fashioned family wedding in church, embarked upon with the utmost seriousness and sincerity, and conveying something a good deal more than the bare minimum in a registrar's office. I believe – as we all do – in taking solemn promises seriously; and in the case of marriage vows (as with so many moral issues) it also makes sound practical sense that a couple confine their sexual favours to one another. But I do *not* believe that Christian marriage is totally indissoluble in all circumstances; I have doubts whether it should be described as a sacrament (it is certainly not a form of magical spell); and my basic argument is that the Church should be very careful against claiming too much for itself, because over the centuries its motives for taking an interest in marriage have been distinctly shifty. If nothing more, I should like you to leave here with some idea of the rubble upon which the foundations of Christian marriage are built.

In a rather large nutshell: the Old Testament (which is essentially Jewish, of course) presents marriage as an instrument for preserving the clan – in particular, the husband's clan. Jesus tightens up the rules against divorce and stresses the personal commitment, the personal merger that is taking place. But he, St Paul and the early Fathers of the Church treat marriage as rather a distraction from the imminent coming of the kingdom. They therefore seek to spiritualize it in a way that had never been attempted before; and for a long time after St Augustine, Christian marriage is seen as a way of sanitizing lust – a necessary evil which can be purified by thinking of it as symbolizing the mystical union between Christ and his Church.

The Council of Trent (which takes us into the mid-sixteenth century) insisted that marriage was inferior to virginity and celibacy. The Protestant Reformers denied that it was a conveyor of grace as a sacrament. Study the marriage service in the Book of Common Prayer of the Church of England and you will notice the same reluctance. If marriage *is* a sacrament, it is the only one in which the parties themselves are the ministers one to the other: the priest is no more than the appointed witness – an agent of society to keep the records and make it legal and official. The priest may like to add a blessing and some good advice, but these are optional extras: he has not married them, they have married each other, and any spiritual implications depend upon the unreserved conviction of the couple.

To quote from the Church of England's Marriage Commission of 1978:

> Marriage is a universal institution which has its origins in nature and society. It does not derive from faith in Jesus Christ and membership of his Church. It is more appropriate to speak of 'a Christian doctrine of marriage' than of 'a doctrine of Christian marriage' . . . To affirm that marriage between the baptised is a sacrament of the Church, instituted by Christ, and that in this sacrament husband and wife are joined together by God in a union which no power on earth can dissolve is, we believe, mistaken. It is not hard to understand how such a development has occurred; nevertheless we are unanimous in our conviction that it strains the witness of Scripture beyond what it can reasonably support.

Incidentally, to this day there are still more remarriages in the Roman Catholic Church than there are in the Church of England; for the Church of England has never taken up the idea of nullity, of apparent marriages that are discovered not to have been valid after all. The Marriage Commission went on to grant that St Paul, by referring to Christ's act of sacrificial love on the cross, had introduced by analogy the idea of a redemptive element into the understanding of marriage. 'Nevertheless', it goes on,

> marriage still belongs properly to the order of creation, and to erect it into a sacrament of the Church is to risk confounding the order of creation with the order of redemption and to suggest too sharp a distinction between 'natural' marriage and 'Christian' marriage . . . We do not accept [it repeats] the view that marriage between baptised Christians is a sacrament and as such indissoluble.

It is also worth noting that, unlike Baptism and Communion, the wedding service is not one of the really ancient liturgies of the Church.

What we think of as Christian marriage has always had a great deal of civil law about it. It began as a contract; and what mattered, and still matters, was the consent of the parties declared before witnesses. This was particularly important where land and property were involved, which is why there was so much fuss in the Dark and Middle Ages about clandestine marriages. The mediaeval Church was deeply involved in the drafting and administration of law (it virtually provided the civil service) but it was not until the eleventh century in the West that the Church's claim to be the exclusive judge of matrimonial cases was established. So far as Britain was concerned, it was another seven centuries before the State began clawing that jurisdiction back; but here in Britain the Established Church was in any case an arm of the State.

How tight a grip the Church got on marriage varied locally. It depended on the authority of the parson and the squire between them, to what extent they went round cracking the whip and driving cohabiting couples to the altar. In wilder and woollier places, the peasantry went on shaking hands, jumping over broomsticks, carrying each other over the doorstep or simply announcing that they were man and wife. It is a relatively late mixture of ensuring legal rights and keeping official statistics that brought us to our present form-filling view of marriage. Incidentally, in Australia you can legally get married without either a civil registrar or by a priest, but with a free-lance Licensed Celebrant, who will compose you a custom-made service and marry you on the beach or in the botanical gardens, if you like.

So while I personally like an old-fashioned wedding, the Church cannot be allowed to get away with pretending that it has always seen things like that, always 'imitated the gospel'. Only recently has it come round to being rather more modest about its own contribution to marriage and to acknowledging that sex is not just an untidy way of making babies, but a communion of love between two persons over and above the possible biological consequences.

But let me try – because it is a fascinating story – to take you into the background of the Mediterranean classical world in which Christian doctrines of marriage first developed. I am indebted here to a host of scholars who have saved me much trouble in doing my own research, notably Robin Lane Fox of my alma mater, New College, Oxford.

It goes without much saying that in the classical world, the dice were heavily loaded against women. Unwanted girl babies were commonly left to die of exposure, while young mothers had a high rate of mortality in childbirth; thus there was often a shortage of young marriageable women, who were snapped up early by older husbands. At least this made it easier for the girls to preserve the virginity expected of them – though not of the men, who sowed their wild oats comprehensively in all directions. Doctors regarded homosexuality (or more commonly bisexuality) as quite normal, though it was seen as a bit ignoble to be the passive partner. Adultery was essentially a female crime – the old double standard of sexual morality goes a long way back.

Formal marriage and divorce were a matter of mutual consent declared before witnesses, in which religion played little if any part. Marriage legitimized children and made for the orderly handing on of property and the preservation of family fortunes. Partly for that reason, what we would regard as incestuous marriage (between uncle and niece, for example) was fairly common in the ancient world. Many men had informal concubines or mistresses, whose children did not inherit. Living together was as common in the second century as it is now. Until the third century, soldiers in the Roman army were forbidden to marry while in service; and there were various forms of racial and social apartheid which applied to formal marriage but not concubinage.

Most women who survived childbirth could expect to be widowed early. At certain periods in the history of Rome they were expected to remarry within two years; but at other periods the problem of what to do with the widows was a serious one which, as we shall see, became particularly severe among the Christian community: looking after widows was probably the major welfare problem of the early Church.

When you think of how the pagan gods carried on in the ancient myths you will assume, rightly, that there was no question of sex being regarded as in any way sinful among the pagans. You were expected to abstain for a day or two before attending some of the great shrines, and some of the cults were served by celibates or virgins. You will think immediately of Rome's Vestal Virgins, but they were chosen and dedicated before they were ten, and they were free to marry after their thirty-year term of office; there was no question of their making a voluntary lifelong sacrifice after the manner of Christian religious. A few of the Stoic philosophers thought abstinence might be a good idea, but it never really caught on; indeed, ancient medicine was firmly convinced that failure to 'have it off' regularly (if you will pardon the expression) was one of the commonest causes of ill health in both sexes. There was, incidentally, a flourishing school of primitive Freudian analysts – headed by one Artemidorus of Daldis – devoted to analysing the meaning of erotic dreams. About the only people who seriously abstained were athletes, who took a rather Hindu view of sex as a loss of vital energy.

I cannot emphasize too strongly that, comparted with all this, the early Christians were trying to live in a totally different world of sexual morality. Attempts to explain Christianity as a development of pagan customs – as borrowing a bit from this and that mystery cult – simply do not make sense. Obviously its roots were in Jewish tradition, and no people were more outraged by, and resistant to, Graeco-Roman practices than the Jews: for example, they were appalled by infanticide and the exposure of unwanted children, and they regarded adultery as equivalent to murder, as also the marriage of brothers with sisters. As for homosexuality – the example of Sodom showed it as bringing physical devastation as well as moral damnation not just to individuals but to the entire community.

All of this the Christians took over, and proceeded to go further still, particularly as regards divorce and remarriage. No question of the early Church going along with the spirit of the times: it spat in that spirit's face and insisted on rigours practised by virtually no one else.

The world of Jesus was almost as liberal with divorce as ours is. But Jesus himself went flatly against it, indeed it is doubtful that he allowed any exception at all. He is not quoted explicitly on the remarriage of widows, except to say that it just will not apply in the life to come. But St Paul is pretty scathing about it and thinks that church leaders should marry only once; as a result of which the early councils of the Church banned twice-married Christians from holding office. The general rule was that although the husband of an adulterous wife could remarry, the wife of an adulterous husband could not; in short, good Christians ought not to remarry under any circumstances, and widows who remained single were admired for relying solely on God. Christian theologians agreed that natural sex was to be tolerated for one reason only, the procreation of children, and primitive versions of birth control were denounced as the sort of beastly things that heretics like the Gnostics did. To quote one modern authority: 'From the very beginning, Christianity considered an orderly sex life to be a clear second best to no sex life at all.' Had not Jesus stated that at the resurrection there was to be neither marrying nor giving in marriage? So why not start now, or rather never begin, by embracing virginity or at least sexless cohabitation? For the second coming, resurrection and judgement, might happen at any moment.

All the same, human nature obstinately remained human nature. Paul had a wife, Peter had a wife, and it is reasonable to assume that most if not all Jewish apostles had wives. Celibacy was not demanded of the Christian ministry for at least three centuries; nor could you be a priest at all if you were a eunuch. So where did this elevation of virginity come from? Only from the gospel picture of Jesus himself and, in a rather mysterious way, of his mother. Jesus, it seems, never married; he even advised his followers to hate their families and become equal to the angels.

We know from the letters of St Paul that quite early on there were Christians, even married couples, trying to copy the angelic example and think only of God. Better to marry than to burn, said Paul, but best of all not to get mixed up in the sexual game in the first place. There were some puritans who argued that the man in the parable who excused himself from the lord's feast on the grounds that 'I have married a wife and cannot come' was indicating the rule that married men should be excluded from communion altogether.

Jesus, then, was seen as teaching that virginity and celibacy were the road to becoming angels at the resurrection. Paul, too, saw them as the best preparation for the coming end of the world. Moreover, sexual innocence was seen as a way of reversing the fall of Adam and Eve: if sex and marriage had helped to bring death into the world, the final defeat of death would surely be hastened by suppressing sex and marriage. Christians were trying to get back to paradise as it was before the fall and, by practising virginity, to turn their eyes upon God alone.

Inevitably, there were problems. True, women were thus relieved of the perils of childbirth. But many parents still felt that the best way of saving their daughters from the sins of premarital sex (quite apart from shifting them off the family expenses) was to marry them off at an early age – medically, far too early. Thus, to become a bride of Christ must have been quite a relief. In some early Christian churches, widows and virgins were seated separately. A very dim view was taken of virgins who changed their minds and got married or took lovers; virginity was for life, not for a limited period. It is interesting to note, however, that in the eyes of some early theologians the greatest possible merit was earned by married couples who renounced sex and were deemed to have become 'virgins by virtue' and not just 'by innocence'. And one reason why I say this is interesting is that in the United States renunciation is becoming fashionable again – as is virginity – almost rivalling vegetarianism for trendiness. How intriguing that customs adopted long ago for religious reasons should now be taken up once more for scientific ones.

Still, the difficulties remained. Early Christian widows were encouraged not to remarry, but who was going to support them? Rather similar problems confronted the dedicated virgins; and while there was a Jewish tradition of caring for widows in the community, ageing spinsters pledged to stay that way were treated with much less sympathy.

There were virtuous bachelors and widowers among the Christians who gathered small households of these ladies around them, and very useful they could be if you could afford them. The ideal candidate for such trusteeship was the bishop or priest; and thus we might trace the origin of the convent with its chaplain, the Catholic bishop with his attentive retinue of nuns, the Catholic priest with his devoted housekeeper and his reluctance to do the washing-up or even make himself a pot of tea . . .

St Paul had some words of advice to Corinthians who began to fancy their resident virgins: marry them, or at least marry them off, before you cannot stand it any longer. The ladies' status was dressed up in concepts like imitating the angels, reversing the catastrophe of the fall, and becoming brides of Christ; and this helped to protect them, for to seduce such a woman would be to commit adultery against the Lord. There was also much discussion by later authorities of how to deal with unholy dreams; severe fasting was agreed to be beneficial to both sexes, as well as encouraging visions of a less carnal sort.

Robin Lane Fox emphasizes that 'this esteem for virginity was something entirely new', which 'owed nothing to pagan example or the mood of the times'; that 'it became a distinguishing feature of Christian life . . . and has survived ever since wherever the faith takes root . . . Nothing in pagan religiousness compared with it.' And though it baffled the pagans, it also much impressed them with its dignity and discipline.

But we are really talking about a Christian doctrine of sexuality, over and above marriage; and it was a doctrine rooted in the belief that the world was shortly going to come to an end; that Christians ought to concentrate on that and purify themselves for it; indeed, if the world was going to end shortly, what was the point of marrying to indulge in sexual activity and produce children? So long as the Church was a tiny, gathered minority – more like a religious order than a cross-section of society – it was not so strange that it should regard reproduction as an inferior activity. As the centuries went by, the Church simply had to accommodate itself to the fact that marriage was not going to go away; at the very least it had to ensure that Christian families were not corrupted by 'marrying out' with pagans, and that the priesthood at least stuck to its ideals. Not that even this was easy: both Eastern and Western Churches found themselves in a position where celibacy was observed by the dedicated who became monks and bishops, while the parish priesthood (the secular clergy) could and did marry. One reason why the Roman Church eventually enforced clerical celibacy was that some corrupt clergy were leaving church property to their children and treated their livings as family heirlooms.

I am simply not learned enough to go into the history of how Christianity developed from a community religion, with elders and welfare officers and a bishop-preacher here and there, into a clericalized one with a strict hierarchy and a very formal distinction between clergy and laity. But once that was established you can see how the liturgy was unlikely to take a particularly human view of marriage, or even to attach great importance to it at all: it was a rather beastly thing the common people insisted on doing. With greater families it remained, as it always had been, essentially a civil contract involving property and requiring the Church's help for documentary reasons as much as anything else.

And yet even the common people hankered after ceremony. They insisted on coming to the Church for its blessing, in the hope, perhaps, that it would protect them from evil and prosper the enterprise. Inevitably a theology of matrimony develops – you can take it back to Genesis ('It is not good for the man to be alone . . . Be fruitful and multiply'), through the ramifications of the Old Testament to Jesus and Paul, where this strangely ambivalent attitude sets in and Paul (in a most unJewish way) declares 'a man is better off having no relations with a woman'. He did not actually say a man would be damned if he did have them, but he certainly thinks such a man would be handicapped.

To the Middle Ages, marriage is presented by the Church as the only way to justify a sexuality which has been infected by sin. 'A lawful remedy for concupiscence', it was called. St Augustine of Hippo (who had been quite a busy lad in his day) ended up regarding sex as an activity for animals, a mere breeding function, polluted by lust and inflicted on us by original sin. People like Augustine were, I believe, influenced partly by those ancient Gnostic and Manichean heresies which regarded the flesh as evil and only the spirit as capable of good, and partly by Greek rationality. They hated the loss of self-control and dignity that sexual activity risks.

So the ambivalence went on. Abelard thought marriage was 'not meritorious for salvation but is allowed because of incontinence'. But when heretics like the Albigensians condemned marriage altogether, the Church felt obliged to endorse it as a good thing after all, and to proclaim it a true sacrament – but not until as late as 1439. To the Protestant Reformers, it was no such thing; the State, not the Church, was deemed to have supreme authority over marriage. Divorce could be accepted as the lesser of two evils. Back came the Catholic Council of Trent saying exactly the opposite, but still affirming the following: 'If anyone says that the married state surpasses that of virginity or celibacy, and that it is not better to remain in virginity or celibacy than to be united in matrimony – let him be Anathema.' There speaks the voice of St Paul and the celibate clergy: getting married is put in much the same category as registering as a drug addict.

But I do not mean to be beastly to the Church by rubbing its nose in ancient documents that are no longer really relevant. Vatican II does drop the old insistence that the begetting of children has to take priority over the mutual love of husband and wife. It accepts as equally valid the idea of what it calls 'the true practice of conjugal love' bringing husband and wife simultaneously closer to each other and to God. The Council did, I think, move towards the secular notion that today people get married and stay married basically because they love one another. The Council talks no longer of a contract but of a covenant: that is, of something that has to be created and maintained mutually, not enforced legalistically.

And (what is really vital to a Christian doctrine of marriage) Vatican II emphasizes that for marriage to be sacramental – that is, an outward and visible sign of God's love – there must be an informed and conscious commitment of faith. It is not enough for the couple to be baptized. Catholic marriage (I would say Christian marriage) is not just a union of baptized Christians but of faithful, convinced and believing Christians. It is an expression of their faith. You have got to enter into it; you cannot just be sprinkled with it.

One could wish – one always does – that the Church would say what it means with precision. But then, if you are too precise it makes it all the harder to change – sorry – *develop* your teaching later. I think progress is being made, if not always at the highest levels, but I hope you can see now why it remains so difficult.

The real experts in this field, like Jack Dominian and his colleagues, know and can tell better than I how the whole context of marriage has changed since the days of the early Church –

health and life expectancy, family structure, the economic roles of the sexes and so forth. How can a Church (or churches), looking to ancient traditions for stability, adjust to these changes, even supposing that they ought to make adjustments? It is even harder when you recall what those traditions are and the values they assume, how long they have endured, the reluctance with which ground has been shifted. And some of you may be moved to ask: are not the old conservative values being proved right at last? If only that high, sacramental seriousness had been observed! If only youthful chastity, monogamy and fidelity – as taught by the Church – had been heeded, we would not be in the mess we are in today!

But that is where we are; and if the Church is claiming that this is because it was ignored, why did it lose its grip, particularly in the field of sex and marriage? I have been trying to suggest that sex and marriage were never subjects that the Church was very keen to come to grips with; for most people, they have always been about the most interesting things in life, but not for the Church. I do not deny that, from the very beginning, the Church had some teachings on sex and marriage which were radical, wholesome, healthy and morally right. But very soon the Church became convinced that marriage and sex were regrettable distractions from what really mattered. Worse than that, they were tainted with sin, and the professional Christian – the dedicated religious – should have nothing to do with them at all. It really took a very long time, perhaps as much as a thousand years, for the idea to dawn in theological and clerical minds that human love (sexual love) was not merely a brutish and distasteful act, necessary for the continuance of the species, but only acceptable in civilized company when sanitized in metaphysical wrappings and made to symbolize something else; not that, but an express and fully human gift of God to be welcomed with joy and not put down with shame. In that sense, a sacrament; but not one that needs an ordained priest to administer it. A priest or minister can (and too often does) turn the wedding ceremony into his solo turn, but there is no place for him in the nuptial bedchamber.

Even if he does want to be helpful in a less obtrusive way, as a counsellor of couples who are in trouble, I have to say that I fear the Church's powers to help are fairly limited. I believe I am right in saying that church-married people divorce at much the same rate as the rest. The Church cannot, even if it wanted to, frighten people into staying together by threats of excommunication and hell fire; and has little if any influence over the many factors which batter at married life today.

So is there any point in getting married in church any more? Not if you imagine that you are being administered some sort of magic spell which will verily lead you not into temptation but deliver you from evil. There is, however, a great deal to be said for standing up in public and saying 'This is how we mean things to be' and for inviting family and friends to be there saying 'We are behind you – and before God'. It shows a seriousness, it makes a commitment, it concentrates the mind. And if you are a religious person, then an extra layer of significance is added to it all, an extra seriousness – as it should be, I think, to everything the religious person does.

Talk delivered at the Annual General Meeting of the Central Middlesex Marriage Guidance Council on 19 November 1986.

9
Boredom

My theme is boredom; and the story of the forbidden fruit, Eve, the serpent and the expulsion from Eden. Now what is the connection? I suggest that the real reason Eve ate that apple is that she was bored – bored stiff. Just think of it: all day long in paradise; no gardening to do, no clothes to make, no meals to cook; Adam out all day naming the animals ('I'll call that bird a Duck – because it's got a face like a Duck-billed Platypus') – or at least, that's what he *said* he was doing. Eve was the original bored housewife. I suppose she could have gone swimming in those four rivers, the Pison, the Gihon, the Hiddekel and the Euphrates; but diving and splashing has its limits. Not even any children to look after, at that point. I would not give Eve more than a week before she started going around the bend with boredom. So what about that tree with the 'Hands Off' notice on it?

But *which* tree? If you read the first chapters of Genesis very carefully, you will notice there are *two* trees involved: the tree of life *and* the tree of the knowledge of good and evil. It is the fruit of this *second* tree ('a tree to be desired to make one wise') that Eve consumes; and God throws them out of the garden 'lest they take *also* of the tree of life and live forever'. The Bible presents us with the picture of a distinctly jealous God who does not want men to become, like himself, both wise *and* immortal (which seems a little unfair).

We all know what happened. Adam and Eve ate the forbidden fruit and started up the fashion industry. Sex was invented as a kind of punishment (something the Church is still hung up about), and work was invented for much the same reason. Our ancestors were kicked out of Eden, and (as the ancient carol puts it) 'So our ruin did begin'. Also all kinds of thrilling adventures like surfing, climbing Mount Everest, sailing the Atlantic single-handed and building the Albert Hall: none of which would have been open to us if Adam and Eve had behaved and kept their fingers off that forbidden fruit.

But the fact of the matter is, they were bored in paradise, rather as (I suppose) we would be bored with the conventional idea of heaven. Who wants to play the harp all day, singing 'Holy, holy, holy'? If heaven really were like that, I bet there would be a heavenly serpent around whispering 'Why not sing some different words? Why not a protest song?'

But for all its hangups, the Genesis story does give us the link between sin and free will. The Lord God must have known perfectly well what was going to happen; after all, he gave Adam the power of choice when he let him name the animals. God just was not going to *make* it happen. We can see now that men and women without the free will to love or reject God's will for them would have been worthless puppets, compelled not only to choose good, but to choose the best. And what makes life so fascinating is that mostly our choices are not between good and evil, but between a whole range of possibilities stretching from the best to the worst by way of fairly good, not so good, fair, indifferent, poor and absolutely lousy.

And yet the popular moan is 'It's boring'. A sophisticated A-level version of that is 'It simply isn't relevant'. Oh dear! All these choices, all this variety (especially of people) around us, and we think it's boring. And bored people get into trouble, not only because trouble can be exciting, but because if there is nothing to push against – no resistance or response to what we do – we get the feeling we do not exist. I am told that if you suspend someone in a darkened tank of warm water, just floating in space with no reference points to see, hear or feel, they get just such a feeling of annihilation. You have to push against something in order to exist. If man were God's puppet, suspended on strings, with no choice but to do the best, then man would not exist as man. We need evil, we need sin, we need disobedience; so the serpent performed a valuable function, and ought to be one of our heroes.

You will detect there a touch of heresy, I hope. But it seems to me that, having made us with free will, God must be prepared to take the consequences. Actually, in the crucifixion, he did. Christians would say he provided a mechanism for the forgiveness of sins, if only we have the wit to recognize it and use it. However, you may be getting bored.

The classic remedy for boredom is activity, especially work. This is a peculiarly British obsession (or used to be) and we despised the Latin and Oriental races for not sharing our passion for it. Underlying this passion, however, the ruling classes of Britain have always been terrified that if the lower orders were *not* kept at work, they would get drunk, take to burglary and riot in the streets. Until comparatively recent times, hours of work were kept long, holidays to a minimum, and labour-saving processes discouraged. Otherwise, it was feared, idle hands would be found work by the devil.

Work, then, has been exalted and protected almost regardless of what it is: soul-destroying (like a production line, or an office filing system), or body-destroying (like the manufacture and sale of arms to countries which ought to be spending their money on the tools of life). Plainly, we have to earn our living as a nation; but Christians believe we have an immortal soul as well as a mortal body. To argue that any work is better than nothing – that if we do not do it, someone else will – is to justify the slave trade.

Incidentally, while I am not for one moment defending the present levels of unemployment, I think it is worth noting that this country has not gone up in flames. Can it be that the lower orders are actually better than the ruling classes have always supposed? That it is not necessary to sort out nuts from bolts all day in order to have some self-respect? I will not press the argument too far – there may be worse trouble ahead – but even marching from Liverpool to London in an orderly manner shows a good deal of self-respect.

But I would not have you think I am always in sympathy with complaints of boredom. They *can* mean 'I can't be bothered to do any thinking – in fact I'm lazy!' Or they can mean 'I demand instant success: I've been in this job six months and they still have not made me the boss!' There is a pernicious cult of quick results, encouraged by (among others) politicians. It goes hand in hand with single-issue politics and the refusal to compromise. Compromise, of course, is terribly boring; but it is usually the path to life rather than to death and destruction. And because it involves having to relate with our fellow men and women, it is actually rather interesting. There is nothing more boring than our solitary selves.

And yet we cannot altogether escape ourselves, even by turning on the television or putting on a record to drown the silence. Eve, of course, had neither: while Adam was out on his zoological duties, there she was with nothing but the serpent-in-her-head. And it told her to stand up and be a woman; frankly, I do not blame her for what she did. The trouble was that to her, God was someone outside, like a policeman on the beat. She had not learnt to listen for the God within. And though it is difficult, the only way to avoid the boredom of the empty self is to develop the inner conversation between oneself and God; or between oneself and the God in others. We are often too much locked up in ourselves. We assume, crazily, that we have too little in common to understand each other; and so we become closed, instead of open to each other. In fact each one of us is fearfully and wonderfully made; even your neighbour is as interesting as you are. But perhaps I have gone on too long. The organist can wake up now.

Sermon delivered at Charterhouse on 7 June and Eton on 14 June 1981.

10

Wrestling with God

In the thirty-second chapter of Genesis, Jacob wrestles all night with a mysterious stranger who will not identify himself. Dawn approaches, and the stranger, anxious not to reveal his face to the light, asks to be released. Even though the encounter has crippled him, Jacob refuses, saying 'I will not let thee go, except thou bless me'.

'Thou hast power with God . . . and hast prevailed', confesses the stranger. And he blesses Jacob, and departs.

Then Jacob calls the place Peniel – the face of God – for he says 'I have seen God face to face and my life is preserved'. The incident is usually described as 'Jacob wrestling with the angel', but it is very clear his antagonist was no mere angel. It was God himself, and the story seems to be an early attempt, antedating Moses on Sinai, to explain the special relationship between Jehovah and Israel. For me it is also one of the crucial images of our faith, as thrilling and mysterious as the burning bush, the still small voice, the valley of dry bones, the empty tomb.

What that story of Jacob means to me is this: it symbolizes not merely the struggle we have to know God, but the battle we have to put up against him if our life is to be preserved. We have to contend with God to prevent him crushing us. We have to contend with him, to wrestle with the Scriptures, in order to survive – even though it may cripple us. We shall not defeat him, any more than Jacob did, but that is not the point. It is an answer to our question that we seek. And if we struggle manfully, though in the dark, we may in the end see God's face and win his blessing. That is what drives us on. We can do no other. There is a case against God and we demand to know his defence.

After much thought I am persuaded that there are some things that must be said in the Church, and answered, if the entire faith is not to be marginalized by the world as an irrelevant hobby, a minority pastime; if it is not to be trundled off into back alleys by those who think they can keep it alive by embalming it, either by bandaging it up in Scripture, or by pickling it in sacraments. Both have their roles to play; but I detect a hankering for unreasonable certainty, when all we can hope for (I believe) is a reasonable uncertainty.

I suppose I am calling for a kind of Christian revisionism. This has been going on in academic theology for fifty years and more: but it has still not trickled down into popular religion, which remains amazingly conservative and evasive. Time and again, we fall back in church upon images which are weary and hollow, yet never questioned: Saved by his precious blood – Three in One and One in Three – On the third day he rose again from the dead – Creator of heaven and earth . . . What can they mean in this day and age? I am not saying they stand for untruths; but what truths *do* they now stand for? To cite the old Quaker challenge: What canst *thou* say?

I shall be told that the true faith is sure and unchanging. But I do not think Christianity would have come down to us at all if that had been so. It is ridiculous to pretend that Christians have always had the same picture before them. It is the development of the picture, its ability to alter its style and reveal different details to every age, that has kept it before us – not that nothing has ever changed.

So there are some of us who have to say that the Bible is *not* the unvarying truth, that there is no simple gospel, no inviolate apostolic succession, either – and that Jesus is not the self-evident final solution, but assumes the role of our partner in the long night's struggle.

Now, there are many just as conscientious as I who feel no quarrel with God, who find their question answered from the moment they surrender to him – and blessed are they. But others of us – more perhaps than will confess it openly – have a different cross to bear; it may cripple us, but we will not let it go except he bless us.

What I am saying, on behalf of us heretics and dissidents, is that being of the race of Jacob, we cannot simply cry 'Lord, Lord!'; and being of the race of Job, too, we cannot expect the whirlwind to answer us unless we confront it. The answer may be crushing, beyond our comprehension; it may leave us speechless in the end. But remember, it was the Lord who commanded Job 'Gird up thy loins now, like a man . . .', who challenged him to struggle.

I suppose most Christians would rather do battle on the ground of the New Testament than the Old. They are prepared to accept the cruelty and injustice of life, the wickedness and sins of mankind, because they believe it is somehow resolved in the cross. So let us look at the demands not of Jehovah but of Jesus: leave your family and follow me; sell all you have and give to the poor; take no heed for the morrow; love one another, and the stranger as yourself; save your life by losing it.

But if Jesus were to turn and say 'Follow me!', would you do it? Would I? Would I drop everything and do just that? Or would I be like the rich young man who asked what he should do to be saved, and did not like what he heard?

There is an alternative to shuffling away in embarrassment. It is to stay and wrestle, crying 'I will not let thee go except thou bless me!', and that is what most of us have to do. 'Lord, you made me and you know what I am. You know I have departed from what I should be, and that only your mercy can save me; that I cannot earn my own salvation by any kind of success. Nevertheless, Lord, you must take me as I am.'

Must? The fact is that he does. He rejects none of us that turn to him and confess our need of his blessing. It is there all the time waiting for us, if only we will admit our inability to do without it. And the blessing is grace, which is nothing else than the love of God, undeservedly given, recognized for what it is, accepted and returned in a constant circular flow. That is the blessing, and it transforms us.

The wrestling could, I suppose, be seen as Jacob wrestling with his own conscience, but the idea of God within is only half the Christian story. God comes within *from* without, and the Christian's conscience never wholly comes to terms with those demands to trust God utterly, to abandon the comforts of life, to sacrifice without hope of reward, to become a servant of the poor, the humiliated and the handicapped – in short, to become a person with absolutely no rights, only duties. It there any one of us who can say that those are our spontaneous ambitions? That we accept them with joy? That we do not have to struggle with them as if they were a threat to our natures?

What do I say if Jesus turns upon me and makes demands like that? Quite frankly, I say, 'Lord, I know that I ought to, but I cannot because I do not want to. In the language of the Church, I am a fallen, sinful man, and I am afraid there is something in me that needs the world's satisfactions in order to keep going. If I actually gave up all those things you want me to give up, I should have to become someone else, and at my age that frightens me.

'And there is one further point, Lord, which is really the heart of the matter: I am not in your class. You tell me to love my neighbours; but they are mostly the same publicans-and-sinners class as myself, and frankly I will not claim to set myself apart from them. If I can do a bit of good in your name, that is where I shall do it; not in the wilderness with a select handful of holy men.

'I know this sounds like an excuse to carry on drinking and making love (incidentally, Lord, how serious are you about celibacy and all that?). Speaking for myself, your gospel – badly compromised, I know – just about helps me to pull through without total disaster. But I have not the nerve to go the whole hog and follow you all the way. Yet I will not let thee go except thou bless me . . .'

And there is a further reason for my obstinacy. Many of my friends are Jews; some are Hindus, Muslims, Sikhs; and yet others are humanists and unbelievers. I cannot believe that our heavenly Father regards them as being lesser children of his. Can it be that in the life hereafter they will be lost, while pious Christians will be saved? That would seem to me outrageous. For most of us are only Christian by accident of birth.

Whenever I talk like this, I am presented with the gospel of John: 'I am the way: no man comes to the Father except through me.' But that is a proposition which I just will not accept, when expressed in those cruel terms; either Jesus did not say that, or he did not mean what the fundamentalists say he meant by it.

Now I accept that Jesus is God; though what I mean by that is certainly not what a conservative evangelical would mean by it. And I can accept that the Scriptures were divinely inspired – though again my definition would be a liberal one. I might even agree that the Christian faith is eternal truth. Those things I would claim to know by experience. But I am talking of religious experience and using religious language, not the language of mechanics or pharmacology or even history. And once we appreciate the relationship between religious language and religious experience, it becomes hard to denounce another religion as false. This is not to say that they are all the same, for that would be to brush aside the variety of religious experience: trouble breaks out whenever we try to insist that other people must share our experience.

Unless we engage in some particular religious tradition, few of us are likely to penetrate far below the surface of the spiritual life, or to have anything we can usefully say to anyone else. What we say will be couched in the terms of a mythology: a system of stories (not necessarily untrue) and metaphors and similes, a kind of poetry. This will be equally true of other religions; and if only we can admit our common limitations, the partiality of our visions of God, we may be able to acquire a less selfish approach to the truth about him.

So it seems to me that Christians should understand the saying 'I am the way, the truth and the life' less selfishly. The disciples have asked Jesus how they are to get to his Father's kingdom, and he tells them: 'It is hard, but on the right track you will always find me waiting. Anyone who comes to unity with God will have been following a path which is mine.'

It is tempting to try and play safe by imitating the first disciples literally. But can we possibly do so? For we do not live in their world, and we cannot work out our situations in their terms. We have theology today precisely because neither the Gospels nor the Creeds even contemplate our situations. You can study them in vain for consistent theories of Christology, the Trinity, salvation, the Church, the priesthood, sacraments. And who knows what Jesus would have taught about nuclear war, democracy, economics, birth control, abortion or the mass media? We have to wrestle with them. We have to protest that God has crippled us and still not blessed us. But we must not let him go.

Like Jacob, from thenceforth known as Israel, we have to continue our pilgrimage. And you will remember that it took Jacob to some strange places, and that it was not until many generations later that his descendants took possession of the promised land. But it was on that night of blind struggle, of refusal to surrender, of insistence upon knowing the unknowable, that Jacob was blessed.

So may it be.

The University Sermon, delivered at St Mary-the-Virgin, Oxford, on 29 January 1984.

11

Peace without and peace within

1. Peace without

To outsiders, The Religious Society of Friends (better known as Quakers) often seem rather vague about what they believe. They tend to start by telling you what they do *not* believe. This is because they are rather suspicious of the word 'believe' in itself. We do not want it to mean 'I say you must agree with this' or 'You cannot come in unless you know our password' or 'You must behave as if this were true, even if you doubt whether it is'. In heavenly matters, Quakers refuse to bind themselves to any earthly authority – whether it be the Church or the Bible; what is essential to them is their direct experience of the will of God, which experience we are careful to check with each other and with the traditions of our Society. And for 300 years, Quakers have been absolutely firm about one thing if nothing else: what we call the Peace Testimony.

Let me quote from a document presented by the Quakers to King Charles II in the year 1660, and entitled *A Declaration from the Harmless and Innocent People of God, called Quakers:*

> We utterly deny all outward wars and strife and fightings with outward weapons, for any end, or under any pretence whatever; this is our testimony to the whole world. We certainly know and testify to the world that the Spirit of Christ, which leads us into all truth, will never move us to fight and war against any man with outward weapons, neither for the kingdom of Christ, nor for the kingdoms of the world.

May I underline two things here: that in the eyes of the first Quakers, wars of religion were just as forbidden as wars of politics or economics; and that while those Quakers were renouncing 'outward' wars and weapons, they were not denying the necessity of conflict and struggle. Pacifists are sometimes rightly accused of being 'soft on evil', of dodging conflict and confrontation. There may sometimes be good reason for doing so. But virtuous people must not do nothing all the time. They must have the courage, when the time comes, to face conflict squarely, as our Lord did. That good may come out of conflict is part of the essential message of the crucifixion–resurrection event.

Quaker pacifism arose during the English Civil War, when the pressures and temptations to take up arms – and the results of refusing to do so – were very heavy. But Quakers did always refuse, and suffered the consequences in vast numbers, 450 of them dying in prison. So it is not surprising that Quakers often speak as if they were the original pacifists. This, however, is not quite true. Quite apart from the very earliest Christians, we must look to the year 1221, when St Francis of Assisi laid it down for his followers that 'You are not to take up deadly weapons, nor bear them against anyone'. This, of course, outraged the feudal authorities, who expected to conscript anyone they chose to fight their wars and did not see why some holy man should be able to go around exempting his own followers. Nevertheless the rule was confirmed by the Pope, Honorius III, and there it stands: an order of men and women pledged to pacifism more than 400 years before George Fox and his Quakers. Which is why I, a Quaker pacifist, now look to St Francis to come to my asistance.

I am to speak to you today of peace in two dimensions: without and within, in the world and in the spirit. They are connected, and yet can be quite separate. I have seen men who were at peace on the battlefield; yet surely it is a sin to be content with one's private peace if cruelty and destruction are raging about us. How to maintain the links? I hope to find the answer in the great prayer of St Francis; each phrase of which (as I understand it) has its meaning both in terms of world peace and in terms of the personal peace of every individual.

Lord, make me an instrument of your peace:
Where there is hatred, let me sow love;
Where there is injury, pardon;
Where there is discord, union;
Where there is doubt, faith;
Where there is despair, hope;
Where there is darkness, light;
Where there is sadness, joy;
For your mercy and truth's sake.
O Divine Master, grant that I may not so much seek
To be consoled as to console,
To be understood as to understand,
To be loved as to love,
For it is in giving that we receive,
It is in pardoning that we are pardoned,
It is in dying that we are born to eternal life.

Notice that through all this there runs the strong, unifying thread of service, service, service – of looking away from self to the good of others – a thread of activity, even of action, not of passivity (which of course is not at all what pacifism is about).

So let us see how this great prayer – this prayer of 'active service', you might say – can illuminate our attitude towards exterior peace.

First we are to be *instruments* of God's peace: we are to offer ourselves for his use in establishing his peace. But how are we to know what he wants us to do? And what is his peace in a world which we know is fallen and which seems doomed to discord? Well, the answers are not going to be easy or palatable, and the details will vary from person to person; but I believe there is only one way to find them. It is not by rushing about signing on for every march or demonstration we hear about; it is by prayer, and prayer is not pestering God on one's knees for five minutes every morning and every night – prayer, above all, is listening and listening constantly. It means learning to open oneself, still oneself, tune in to God's wavelength and recognize his signals. I shall try to say more about this when we come to interior peace; but what I am trying to say now is that unless we cultivate prayer we shall not know what kind of instrument God wants us to be. It may be he wants us to serve his peace as a teacher, as a parent, as a policeman, a gardener, a priest, a journalist. You may be quite sure it will be as something *active*: he will not just say, I want you to be peaceful and peace-loving and refrain from doing anything lest you do some harm.

And what is his peace? It is a way of life, and as a Quaker I do of course believe that the absence of physical violence is a very important part of that way. I personally am very anxious not to confuse physical violence with other kinds of coercion and oppression: it worries me when people (for example) describe government policies as violence against the poor, or say that 'discrimination against black people is violence' or 'It is violence to deprive the Third World of adequate nutrition'. These things may be callous, cruel, thoughtless, selfish, even evil. But to call them 'violence' is to soften the horrific blows of real, physical violence. There are several things that make violence particularly horrible: once it is unleashed, it is unpredictable, uncontrollable, subject to its own laws. There is no knowing where it will lead. Thus we begin by resisting Hitler, and end four years later dropping the atom bomb on Hiroshima. Violence is nobody's instrument: it makes instruments of people. Violence cancels out and brushes aside all language and reason; it reduces the humanity of those who employ it. Violence is a blasphemy, not only because it involves the destruction of God's creation, but because it is only possible when its practitioners regard their victims no longer as brothers and sisters under God but instead as aliens, as lesser creatures with lesser needs and affections. For all these reasons, I regard violence as the supreme evil, and I find that endorsed by the life and teaching and death of our Lord.

But there are few, if any, people who employ violence for its own sake. Violence is the language of last resort. People do not, I think, really use it to achieve something (for it is a blunt and uncontrollable instrument); they use it, rather, to say something when normal communication has broken down. That is why I think the mass media of communication *can* be, *should* be and sometimes are instruments of peace; because if they get the message right they can avert the use of violence. Violence is always *about* something – I don't believe in so-called 'mindless violence' – so that if we desire that peace in which God's creation is not being destroyed, we have to be attentive to the causes of destructiveness. At the risk of sounding trite: God's peace is not just a matter of stopping wars, but of discerning what causes war and eliminating the causes.

Where there is hatred, let me sow love. Do you, I wonder, hate the Russians? Do the Russians, I wonder, hate the Americans? I should be very surprised if many of us *knew* any Russians to hate; speaking for myself, I do not so much hate the Russians (by which I mean, I suppose, their leadership) as distrust and disbelieve them. To be frank, I know very little about them (nothing at first hand) and I cannot really claim to understand them. On the other hand, having lived in the United States for years, I know scores of Americans and I think I understand them; and although I do not like many of the things their leaders do, I can see why they do them.

This word 'love' can be troublesome: I am sure that Francis really did love; but about the best I can manage most of the time is to care about people, sometimes even to care for them. What I extract from this is that on the personal level I should use my knowledge of Americans to spread understanding of their behaviour, and in order to gain understanding of Russian behaviour I really ought to get to know a few Russians and care for and about them. This is by no means easy; but so long as we allow ourselves to think of 'them' – be they Russians, Americans, Argentinians or Irish – as alien stereotypes, then it will be all too easy for people in power (frightened people, afraid of losing face, perhaps) to get us to treat each other as lesser breeds fit to be bashed. We may not have it in our power to visit Russia, America or Argentina: but I am surprised how few English people have any first-hand experience of Ireland and the Irish, North or South. If we had more experience of them, there might be less indifference and contempt – more sympathetic concern.

Where there is injury, pardon. There are many virtues which Christians share with the followers of other religions. Qualities like truth-telling, courage, and respect for the weak are widely admired. But one of the virtues which I think is peculiar to Christianity (though often conveniently forgotten) is that of unrequited concession, of unrewarded generosity, of taking the first step back, even if you get mocked for doing so. Politically it is very unpopular, or is thought to be so, being regarded as a sign of weakness. And for that reason, the strong – who could afford to – do not do it, and neither do the weak. I believe that we British, as a nation, give way too little; we pardon those who injure us (for example, Argentina) too grudgingly. In the end, the grass grows over the bomb craters, the newpapers turn to another story and life goes on as if we had pardoned; but in fact we have not. All that has happened is that the fire has burnt itself out and become cold. The face that has been saved is still the same old mask. We have missed, yet again, the opportunity of taking the sting out of death by enacting the prayer 'Father, forgive them, they know not what they do'. Instead, we return evil for evil and bomb for bomb until somebody wins and all is lost.

Where there is discord, union. How can we bring the nations of the world together, in union, in ways that will reduce and not increase the divisions among them? Formal arrangements for encouraging unity often seem to have the opposite effect. Has the United Nations really increased the harmony of nations? Have the Olympic Games, international sport, world broadcasting, multinational companies and foreign travel really done more good than harm? Part of the trouble, it seems to me, lies in the very nature of the systems in which human beings feel themselves caught up. It happens on both the national and the international level. People feel themselves the helpless victims of the companies they work for, of the trade unions they are obliged to join, of the political parties which they have to vote for, of the economic markets which buy and sell their products. On the wider scale, we are carried along by national interests, regional and ideological commitments, alliances which are said to be acting on our behalf – though we cannot remember when they actually consulted us.

Let me seize upon that word 'union': what is it that can unite us with our presumed enemies? Not a denial that there really are conflicting interests, disputed territories, injuries and injustices – these are not illusions. But we are all human, and believers would insist that we are all brothers and sisters under the parenthood of God. Goodness knows, religion has itself been a terrible cause of discord in the past; but the Holy Spirit does make progress, and it is now possible for believers of all faiths to find union in belief itself. The fashionable word is dialogue, or convergence. I am not advocating any worldwide melting together of faiths; I am not even terribly interested in the engineering of Church unity. But I do believe that there is now a better chance of finding human unity through religion than there is through politics or economics, the gods that really have failed.

Where there is doubt, faith. There we have it again. I do believe that the combating of atheism, with its totally unreal fantasies that if only we get the systems right, earth shall be fair and all men wise and good – the combating of that heresy is essential for exterior peace. You cannot, of course, prove the existence of God in the way that you can prove the presence of a cat in the garden. God could not be the God he is if you could prove that he was. You cannot close the circle round him; there must always be a gap for him to vanish through. The trouble is not so much that people do not believe in a supreme being: the trouble is that they see belief as optional, and as being presented on the terms of a discredited Church. If there is a God, and if he is the kind of God we believe in, then peace amongst his creation is his will, and violence amongst his creation is a blasphemy. The instrument of his peace must strive with renewed determination for the knowing and showing of God. At the risk of appearing something of a theological radical; I think it is no good meeting the religious doubts of this age by repeating the old formulas. There must be formulations of faith which make sense today. But here I am straying into the spiritual dimension: there is another sense in which faith must combat doubt if we are to secure peace, and it is reflected in the words:

Where there is despair, hope. The instrument of God's peace must have faith that all shall be well and all manner of thing shall be well. Fundamentally the universe is on our side, if only we will work with it and not against it, if only we will stop telling it to stand aside because we know better what is good for us. If it is not on our side, then life is absurd. But I suggest that we have only to respond to that which is of God in everyone – to speak to it and draw it out – to realize that life is *not* absurd, that there is no need to despair, that even history – which we may be tempted to see as unmitigated disaster – gives every cause for hope. Is it not a hopeful sign that war is now so very unpopular, and no longer a glorious patriotic adventure? That people and goverments feel guilty about despoiling the environment? That they rush to relieve disasters, and at least make excuses for discrimination and persecution, which would have been shrugged off as routine a century ago?

Where there is darkness, light. Faith and hope do cast light, of course. But the peacemaker can cast another sort of light into the darkness: the light of truth, of facts and information. We cannot root out the causes of conflict, we cannot protest against the dangerous things being done in our name regardless of our wishes, unless we know what is going on; therefore we should support free and varied media of information and resist attempts to restrict them. But there are several formidable difficulties, of professional interest to me as a journalist. One is the cult of secrecy in goverment, wrapped up in various cloaks ranging from national security to the right of parliament to know first. Another is that – frankly – we are a country that despises education, and an ill-educated public is bound to get an ill-educated press. Not least, the production of newpapers and broadcasting has now become so expensive that truth has almost been priced off the market. As for the task of the foreign correspondent, when he tries to find out what is happening overseas, he is liable to run up against every form of obstruction from official lying and censorship to pressures upon reporters who send home unwelcome facts. The facts themselves are often hard enough to come by, but they are not by themselves the whole truth: that depends on interpretation, background, understanding, and even sympathy. I think it is the duty of the foreign correspondent, as of the specialist reporter in any field, to put himself in the position of those he is reporting and to explain their point of view – why they have acted as they did, the circumstances and perceptions that led up to it. For it is all too easy for an editorial office to simplify things down to the assumption that all foreigners – or socialists – or trade unionists – are mad, bad and beastly.

What can readers, viewers or listeners do to encourage the light? They should read and listen as widely as they can; beware of relying on a single source of information (though it is worth paying attention to correspondents who have proved themselves over the years) and should always keep in the back of their minds that the reverse of the obvious may be the case: that the strikers *might* be right, that our side *may* have started it, that the bad guys may not be so bad after all.

Where there is sadness, joy. I see this as springing from resurrection. I see God not only as love but as joy: joy in the creation of new life out of confusion, in the putting behind us of old antagonisms and mistakes and starting again – joy in the opportunity. And in an odd way, this has to begin as utterly one-sided. One has to go forth to meet the world without looking to see if it has a smile on its face, if it is going to meet one half-way. It may not, it may reject one. But still one has to bounce back – with joy out of the sadness – glad to have the chance, yet again, to serve with love; the chance to get out of the slough of despond and renew the effort – consoling, understanding, loving, giving, pardoning – and, if necessary, being crucified for it.

Now, when Francis was criticized for being impossibly radical about giving up wordly possessions, he responded that if you had nothing, there was nothing to quarrel with your fellow men about. The trouble is, of course, that most of us have a great deal that we cannot really dispose of, especially if we have wives and families, a role in the community, a living to make; and when we come to the community, whose possessions include the very island on which we live, it cannot very well abjure them without willing to abolish itself. The great deterrent to national pacifism and unilateral disarmament is the fear that it will mean national suicide. It is all very well to speak of losing one's life in order to save it; but no government would feel it had the right to risk the existence we know for another we do not. Nor would it have that right, in my view, because nothing like a majority of the population would back the gamble. If the pacifist expects the community to recognize his or her conscience, he or she must also recognize the sincerity of those whose conscience requires them to offer resistance to aggression. All we can reasonably demand is that conscience be informed, that as much light as possible be turned upon the darkness.

Let us indulge in a little more icy realism. When we come to understand our opponents, we will not necessarily like what we understand or find it reasonable and acceptable. People are manipulated and incited by wicked leaders; systems develop a momentum of their own and become hard to resist (and that applies to 'us' as well as 'them'). It is a dangerous world and always has been; we cannot make the dangers go away by smiling and breathing 'peace'. We have to realize that peace is pluralist, just as politics and economics and religion are pluralist. There is more than one approach and it is futile to pretend that all the others can be dismissed. We have to take limited negotiation and even deterrence seriously. We have to keep chipping away from every possible direction at once.

Quakers and Franciscans alike call themselves 'Societies'. Friends have been called a lay order within the great Church that is the people of God, and I think most of us have a strong feel of having been called to the Society, of having a vocation. And that is how I feel about my pacifism and its place in the pluralism of peace-seeking: it is a vocation, and it is also a sacrifice and a burden, as surely as a Catholic priest's vocation to celibacy. I am prepared to reason and argue about it, even to justify it: I think, for example, that the growth of total warfare, of terrorism, of arms technology now make it almost impossible for the theory of the just war to stand up any more. But in the end, my pacifism is *my* devotion, my vocation: it is a cross that I must hold up even on the battlefield. Somebody must bear witness to the ideal, which means showing it in action, or else there is nothing left for mankind but cynical calculation. In the end, it is the example of Christ – and that is good enough for me. In the world's eyes, he was a failure: but he did not draw back because people told him the cross 'wouldn't work'.

Thinking back to World War II, many Friends are humbly aware that their pacifism was, in a sense, paid for and protected by those who went out to fight – though, mind you, many Friends did return the compliment with their service as firemen, ambulance staff, whatever they were given as non-combatants. But I hope and believe that there was and is another mysterious sense in which the devoted pacifist is contributing by his devotion to the eternal life of his brothers and sisters, as surely as the monk praying for the sins of the world. I think God needs our love, and needs to know our response to his love, or his work is frustrated. His love *must* will that we love one another, not fight one another. So long as there are enough of us to show that, he surely will not despair of us and finally turn his back.

2. Peace within

In my ramblings about peace in the world, I have tried to train my remarks up the trellis provided by Francis' great prayer 'Make me an instrument of your peace'. I want to use the same structure now for some thoughts about peace in the spirit. For the fact is, there *is* no peace in the world, and there never will be, though that must not discourage us from struggling for it. There will always be fire in the city, but we must strive to keep it under control, to stop it from spreading and destroying us all.

Looked at as a spiritual formula, the prayer of Francis still shows that quality of active service, of selflessness. It does not say 'Give me love, give me pardon, give me faith, hope, light, joy'; it seeks the privilege of being able to sow these gifts among others. It always looks outwards to others, asking not to be consoled but to console, though in the end recognizing that the best way to receive is to give. Make others happy, and you will find yourself bathed in happiness. Love others, and you will find yourself drenched in love and at peace – but not because those others will love us in return: they may, or they may not. Francis is not saying 'Pardon your enemy so that he will pardon you in return'; he is saying 'Pardon your enemy and God will pardon you', or (as I see it) 'The God in you will pardon yourself – you will forgive yourself and be at peace with yourself', and this is terribly important.

To do that, as Francis realizes in his prayer, one has to realize that one can and does love, and is therefore lovable and need not punish oneself. And if one has any religious apprehension at all, one realizes that God too loves one, and that this is the root of all love. The truth about life is love, and the truth about love is that it is God. You can be at one with him, at one with yourself, there is peace – maybe only for a while, but you know that it exists now, that it is real and attainable.

Where there is hatred, let me sow love. I have spoken about hating oneself (which is much more common than most people think), and loving oneself (which, if you take it seriously, is much tougher and less self-indulgent). I often prefer to use the word 'care' rather than love. Caring for oneself is rather like caring for a child – probably a rather difficult teenager whom you know all too well to dote on. To care for that child, you have got to understand its background, its limitations, its strong points and weak; and, of course, you have got to accept it for what it *is* and not keep trying to make it what you would like it to be. Sometimes it goes off on some crazy experiment; but you know that, inside, there is its real, true nature – its best self, which is what God intended it (intended you) to be. Not perfect, but not so bad after all.

The terrible thing about hatred, whether it is hating yourself or hating others, is that it breeds and feeds on itself like some dreadful cancer. And because we know it is wrong, we hate ourselves for hating, and we hide it away and it festers.

One of the oddest things about us is the way we can sit inside ourselves thinking 'I'm terribly deep . . . I'm a well going down to the centre of the earth full of profound thoughts, vibrant emotions, feelings of amazing richness; but this person next to me cannot possibly be like that: they are only six inches deep, almost a cardboard cut-out . . .' (I think this is called solipsism). Well, of course, it is difficult, if not impossible, to enter into other people's experience of themselves and share it; but there is no logical reason to suppose that anyone of us is less self-conscious than another. The difficulty is not just a failure of imagination or empathy; it is also, partly, that we find it difficult to be open to others, to let them look into our own depths. For it could be dangerous – we might be betrayed or laughed at or wounded. And yet, in my experience, people who are at peace with themselves, who are full of love and free from hatred, are usually very open. They do not necessarily go round throwing themselves about in handfuls; but if you want to look into them, they will let you. Whether they are at peace because they are open, or are open because they are at peace, I could not say; but the two go together.

Where there is injury, pardon. 'Forgive us our trespasses as we forgive them that trespass against us.' It follows from the Lord's Prayer that we cannot expect to be at peace with God if we are at war with our brothers or sisters. For a start, they are his children, and he will judge and correct them as he sees fit. It will do us no good at all, and certainly not bring spiritual peace, if we brood over the injuries done us, perhaps become a little proud of them, and allow the cancer of hatred to take root. I am inclined to repeat this clause of Francis' prayer rather quietly; because I do not think it is very healthy to develop a nose for injuries in order to be able to pardon them. Much better, if you can, simply to overlook them, to pretend they never happened. I once knew a man who was unjustly pilloried in a satirical magazine. Word got round, and somebody asked him what he was going to do about it. 'Nothing', he said, 'I haven't read it and I don't propose to. I don't see the point in adding to the world's bitterness. As far as I am concerned, there is nothing to resent or forgive.' I suppose some would say he was cowardly or smug; but was there really any good reason why he should have allowed his peace of mind to be disturbed by mischievous gossip? Of course we cannot dodge all injury, for some we bring upon ourselves, and then we have the difficult task of suffering the pain without the comfort of being able to blame it on others. And we must be able to pardon ourselves.

Where there is discord, union. This is very difficult; for spiritual peace – when the grace is flowing without interruption between us and God – is very rare and subject to constant interference both within and without. If I believe in the devil – which I do not, as I think he is really us, pretending to be him – I would say the devil's most ingenious invention for a long time has been non-stop pop music: oozing out of the ceilings of supermarkets, blaring out of car windows, and now even available in Walkman sets with headphones, so that you can fill your head with discord as you stroll through the summer woods. Even without the music it is hard enough. One of the first things I had to learn when I joined the Quakers and started attending their silent meetings for worship was how to 'centre down', as we say, how to clear my head of my tax problems and stop re-running the scenarios of the past week and rehearsing new ones for the next; how, in the marvellous words of *The Epistle of Privy Counsel*, to clear my mind of my good thoughts as well as my bad ones and think only that I am as I am and he is as he is. Once I can do that, there is a small point at which he and I are one, are in union, for at that point he is me. The problem is to unearth it, to clear away the discord, for that point is very shy and many people cannot even believe it is there.

As for techniques for quelling the discord, I am no spiritual director at all; but I am sure they begin with this learning to love oneself, with convincing oneself that one has a true, lovable self under all the shabby garments we accumulate. We cannot stand too much reality. At best we get a glimpse of God's back, a flash of his face as dawn breaks after the long night's wrestling. The thing is to cultivate an eye for such moments, for they come and go like lightning in my experience. Suddenly the discord ceases and everything clicks into union – and then flies apart again. And the magical thing is, as Francis must have known, that people who get these clicks and flashes pass on something of their effect to those about them; I suppose they are saints.

Where there is doubt, faith. But *has* faith such a good reputation as a bringer of peace? I am not really thinking here of crusades, persecutions and wars of religion; some people's faith disturbs them deeply, inwardly, and brings them no peace. And let us not decry doubt: we shall not reach the truth by avoiding confrontation and conflict. We should know very well that God sometimes absents himself, leaving us to wonder if he is ever coming back: 'My God, my God, why hast thou forsaken me?' I do not, however, think that faith here means an elaborate system of doctrine, either the Holy, Apostolic and Catholic Faith or the old-time Bible-based religion. I think it means what I would call trust. We may have doubts about where God is, what he is, and what he thinks he is up to (if anything); but that he *is*, that he loves us, that he has not forgotten us and will be back again in his own good time, that we can and must trust. We cannot doubt the goodness of God (as Muslims, incidentally, perceive very clearly). Recently I have been asking a long succession of people how they come to terms with unmerited suffering in the world, how they reconcile that with the goodness of God. Surely we deserve something better? Just one of my witnesses – a poet – burst out: 'I'm sick of hearing about what we deserve. We deserve nothing. We don't even deserve to be born. It's a privilege to live for a day.' I think he was right.

Where there is despair, hope. Well, where there is despair there is by definition no real peace, certainly no spiritual peace. But how can one answer it with hope? When everything has gone disastrously wrong, some innocent pipes 'Cheer up – where there's life there's hope!' How can the instrument of God's peace fly in the face of the evidence like that? If he likes, he can preach a little sermon about Holy Saturday and the resurrection and the assurance of life eternal. Thanks a lot, say the sceptics, we were looking for something less drastic. I am not sure that there is; but it seems to me the Christian hope brings with it, or requires, another quality which is less often mentioned, and that is patience, the capacity to wait, like a good servant, without ambition or reproach. Time has speeded up enormously during the past hundred years: whole diseases have been abolished, science fiction has come true, worlds have been turned upside down. Much of this is all to the good, though in some respects our progress is slower than it ought to be. But many things we expect too soon. A great deal of political frustration is due to the fact that politicians promise more than they (or anybody) could deliver. It is not that nothing can be done, but that it will take longer and achieve less than we would like. People still move, they still change, more slowly than machines do, and to make them move faster usually means using the lash, as in that poem of W. B. Yeats:

> Hurrah for the Revolution, and more cannon shot;
> A beggar upon horseback lashes a beggar on foot.
> Hurrah for the Revolution, and cannon come again;
> The beggars have changed places, but the lash goes on.

So we can have our revolution, burning with hope, but the end result will probably be a new despair. It is unfashionable to say this, but peacemakers need to be very patient, for they will have many disappointments and, without patience, their hope may die. To be patient is not to be lazy or to fall asleep; it is to keep pressing forward inch by inch, rather than risking one giant leap. In the world of the spirit it is equally true, and this is one thing that worries me about spectacular conversions: people take a leap out of despair and leave too much empty space behind them. Hope, I think, counsels us to be more patient.

And *Where there is darkness, light*. Spiritual darkness can be of two kinds. There can be the dark night of the soul, which may have to *be* suffered in darkness – one would like to think, with the comfort of trust, that the light has been quenched deliberately by God for his own good reasons. Some great souls may even find a sort of peace in the dark, if they have hope and patience. The eighteenth-century Rhode Island Quaker Job Scott wrote:

> A hope was kindled in me that I should now go forward without meeting such besetments and withdrawings of light as heretofore; for though at times the Lord withdrew from me, yet as His return was not long after, I was ready to conclude it would continue with increasing brightness . . . It is not all calm and sunshine. We have cold as well as heat, darkness as well as light.

But Friends have always known a more sinister kind of spiritual darkness. Hear now George Fox himself recounting, I think, the depths of this own depression:

> I was under great temptations sometimes, and my inward sufferings were heavy; but I could find none to open my condition to but the Lord alone, unto whom I cried night and day. And I went back into Nottinghamshire, and there the Lord shewed me that the natures of those things which were hurtful without were within, in the hearts and minds of wicked men. The natures of dogs, swine, vipers, of Sodom and Egypt, Pharaoh, Cain, Ishmael, Esau, etcetera . . . The natures of these I saw within, though people had been looking without. And I cried to the Lord, saying 'Why should I be thus, seeing I was never addicted to commit these crimes?' And the Lord answered that it was needful I should have a sense of all conditions, how else should I speak to all conditions; and in this I saw the infinite love of God, I saw also that there was an ocean of darkness and death, but an infinite ocean of light and love, which flowed over the ocean of darkness.

Well, the Light of which Fox always speaks is much more than conscience or truth: it is the grace of God. But before Fox can see it, he has to go through the experience of acknowledging within himself the potentiality for all the abominations which (as a born Puritan) he had imagined to be beyond him. It appalled him, but it was not until he accepted it all as part of the human condition which he shared that the light broke through and he felt forgiven. He then went around announcing that he was a man free from sin – for which he was very properly thrown into jail.

So it seems to follow that the light which we are to hold aloft in service to our brothers and sisters is to be borne out of the darkness – our own darkness, which God wills us to recognize. We must not pretend we do not have it in us, but we must know and show that the light flows over it and conquers it. Again, I do not think this light is doctrinal truth. I think it is the grace of God – his unmerited love, received and recognized for what it is and responded to by us.

And so *Where there is sadness, joy.* After that, how could it be otherwise? To all the other clauses in this prayer, I am afraid I have responded rather solemnly and piously. But spiritual peace, at-one-ment with ourselves and with God, surely must produce tremendous, active joy. To turn again to George Fox:

> Now was I come up in spirit through the flaming sword into the paradise of God. All things were new, and all the creation gave another smell unto me than before, beyond what words can utter. I knew nothing but pureness and innocency and righteousness, being renewed up into the image of God by Christ Jesus, so that I say I was come up to the state of Adam, which he was in before he fell.

Well, there is the testimony of a recovered depressive; and when he died, his last words were 'Now I am clear: now I am fully clear'.

In short, he was at peace, both inwardly and outwardly – though I am not pretending for one moment that he compares with Francis in real saintliness. Fox was much loved and admired by his contemporaries, but he could be dreadfully priggish and vindictive and never failed to record when people who crossed him came to a bad end. But he was a man who successfully confronted the violence within himself and within his society and gave to both the answer of peace. As the Lord explained to him, he had to come to terms with his own sinfulness – including his own violence – if he was to understand and speak to the condition of ordinary sinful men and women. So if we are to be instruments of God's peace in the world (and it is in modest ways, the opportunities under our noses, that we can be most effective), we have to begin by establishing peace within ourselves. We have to be frank and recognize that however virtuous we want to be and try to be, we are still perfectly capable of behaving viciously. We cannot resolve the conflict by pretending that our vicious tendencies are not there – by trying to brick them up in oubliettes, as Fox did. I think we have to accept them as our own, as part of ourselves, understand what has gone wrong with them and even try to find useful things for them to do.

That may sound a bit odd, but I am rather attracted by the theory a friend offered me some years ago, that vices are really virtues that have gone too far and got warped: that lust is perverted love, envy perverted admiration, even violence perverted courage . . . I suppose I am under the influence of the optimism about human nature which Quakers tend to show. We tend to begin at the opposite end to original sin, and to view human wickedness through rose-tinted glasses.

Be that as it may, if we are to be convincing pacifists towards others, we have to resolve our battles with ourselves and declare peace with ourselves before we can find the confidence to disarm and present ourselves as a threat to nobody.

As I have tried to indicate, our inner peace – like the outer peace we aim to serve – will not, I hope, be a dull eventlessness. I do not think God wants that, either in our soul or in the world. Evolution, it seems, is the result of a series of challenges, and the challenges must continue if we are to be jolted into discerning God's will. In his *Letters of Direction*, the Abbé de Tourville (who lived from 1842 to 1903) was constantly trying to calm people down and yet maintain their sense of adventure in the world:

> Things go wrong in order to show us that it is God's will that we should change them. That is the real truth . . . I think God keeps the world moving in order to shake us out of our old set shapes and bring us back to more natural ways. That at least is what happens periodically in history. The present day is both very good and very interesting . . . It is not right to groan over the state of the world as if it were lost. What is actually happening is a clash between the old spirit and the new, a clash which is specially noticeable because the old spirit is realising how old it is and how nothing is looked at any longer from its point of view. It is a great struggle of which the issue is never in doubt, a struggle in which that which is coming triumphs over that which has been.

Here is a man who combines a deep inner peace with excitement about the conflicts in the world. He does not see them as disasters, because his peace (though he was in constant physical pain) was rooted in absolute confidence in God's goodness and mercy. He was sometimes quite exasperated with people who would not believe that God loved them just as they were, sins and all. He was not interested in a spiritual peace that involved the sureness of one's *own* goodness – that was a waste of time, quite impossible – one could only be sure that God was not demanding perfection, either. If he was waiting for perfect people to love him, he would never get loved (and I recall here Jesus' fondness for publicans and sinners . . .).

So we should not expect the advance of God's peace in the world to mean the transformation of the nations of the world into passive paragons of virtue. Of course there will be quarrels and conflicts among them – the new ideas battering at the old, and the old resisting – though that does not have to end in violence, any more than every disagreement among individuals must end in fisticuffs. What asserts the peace of God (which, you see, is confidence, trust, certainty of his goodness) is precisely those qualities for which Francis prayed – love, pardon, union, faith, hope, light, joy; and it is the presence of these, not the absence of conflict, that adds up to peace.

How can we be instruments of it? In the end, it is a question of example. It is not a question of peering about us for opportunities to be conspicuous peacemakers, devising ways to manipulate people towards peace. Francis prays for God to seize *him* as an opportunity, to manipulate and use *him*; and in every clause Francis is offering himself in service, as a bringer of the positive to overwhelm the negative – the ocean of light, flowing over the ocean of darkness and death. But we cannot bring these things to the world if we do not have them within us to give. We must start with the interior and work outwards: fill ourselves (or become filled) with love and pardon, joy and the rest, so as to be peace-full. Then you will be an instrument worth using – and who knows what job God will find for it? It has just occurred to me that Francis uses this unaggressive word 'sow' – 'let me sow love'; and the sower is one who casts the seed and passes on, leaving others to reap the benefit.

So, make peace with yourself and with your God, then with your brother and neighbour; and – who knows? – tomorrow, the world.

Two talks first delivered to the Bristol Franciscan Conference in May 1984; revised and abridged for Brisbane Friends in the following year.

12

Coping with depression

I hope it is understood that in talking about depression – by which I mean a severe illness and not just 'feeling a bit sad' – I speak as a lay person and in no way as a medical expert. To be frank, I *dislike* talking about it; I am always afraid that if I re-live it too deeply I shall in fact relapse; but I do this occasionally because I think people need to take depression seriously, and having done so, need to get the message that there is hope. Recently I was given two popular medical books to review, one on depression, the other on bad backs; the editor knew I had suffered from both, and it was quite clear to me that today there is more hope for sufferers from depression than there is for sufferers from bad backs . . .

The only credentials, then, that I have to speak about depression are that I myself am a recovered (like an alcoholic, I hesitate to say cured) depressive; and that as a result of admitting and discussing this two or three times on the air, I have been in touch (mostly by letter) with some two to three hundred other depressives or supposed depressives.

I have no training in any kind of psychiatry or psychotherapy and I must emphasize that I do not try to practise as an amateur therapist myself. I invariably urge people to do what is obvious enough, but evidently very difficult for them: to confide in their GP, and if necessary to seek referral to a qualified psychiatrist. Just to get over that first hurdle is the important thing; and I have no advice to give as between different types of treatment or different schools of psychiatry.

At best I hope to make a few sufferers feel less lonely, less mad, less hopeless. I have tried to hold out my own experience as encouragement – you can get through. But I have always warned that what worked for me may not work for others – for there are important varieties in depression. There is one big point which I have to make (though some good people deplore my making it as a religious person): I am very much afraid there is little point in looking to faith and prayer for relief. In all my contacts I have heard from only two people who claimed to have been healed by their faith. In my experience Christianity is of no help; indeed many find it to be an aggravator of their despair.

Perhaps the best thing I can do now is to outline my own case – or to be frank, how it seems to me today, since I suppose I may be covering up my tracks.

I was born 61 years ago of middle-class parents who were struggling hard to keep up with the Joneses. I had a nanny, and I was an only child, and was sent off to boarding school at the age of eight; not a bad idea in many ways, because I got the company I lacked at home; I was academically bright, and I got an excellent education of its kind. It was also considered very important that I should not be spoilt or given a swollen head. It was the kind of school where one's best was never good enough. Needless to say, I grew up hungry to be spoilt and praised.

My schools were high-pressure scholarship factories and I was expected to excel. Which I did – but I have never run so scared nor worked so hard in my life; coal-miners would have gone on strike if they had been expected to work the hours I was working at the age of twelve – it was child servitude. But I was an extremely *good* boy, and almost died of shame when I got a black mark, which indeed I very rarely did. I had a particular horror of being late for anything.

From the age of fourteen and fifteen I began to experience bouts of that empty blackness, drained of all hope, in which you know (and this is typical) that your apparent success is a fraud; that you will eventually be found out and punished for it, and that, above all, there is no future. You cannot imagine having one; there will not be one for you. Incidentally, unlike some depressives, I do not think that I had any upswing – the manic phase; there was just very hard work.

This went on through my public school, through Oxford. I married when I left Oxford, at the age of twenty-two. I still have the same wonderful wife; one of the things that attracted me to her was that she came of an extended family of seven children, and we have four of our own.

As a broadcasting journalist I had a career which you may judge for yourselves. I have found it fascinating and exciting, but I always felt that I had to run desperately to stay in the same place. The terror of being late (which is a real crime in broadcasting) became an obsession.

As I entered my forties, the black periods increased and deepened, and the conviction that I had committed some nameless crime which 'they' – the pursuing Furies – would unmask, and for which the penalty was death, grew stronger and stronger. But this was not something I could tell anyone – not even my wife – for I knew it would seem nonsense and not be understood.

I was not upset by the death of my father. But my mother's death devasted me. She died before my eyes as I was saying goodbye to her on the eve of leaving for a post in the United States. In fact she had been far from well since my father died, but I felt I had killed her by breaking her heart. It was the supreme violence of murder.

My time in America was a violent time: the assassinations, the black ghetto riots, the war in Vietnam of which I saw a good deal at first hand. I began to write a book on human violence, but broke down in the middle of it as our eldest child married and left home. My GP put the brakes on by prescribing Tryptazol and then referred me to a classic Viennese psychiatrist, who saved me and brought me my Damascus road experience. I simply lay and gabbled my life out, and when I ran dry he would intervene saying 'What I think you are trying to tell me is . . .'. And he was usually right.

It was all to do, of course, with having been taken away from my mother too soon – I had assumed, childishly, as a punishment. So if they did not want me, I did not want them – I would stay away as long as I could to punish *them*, and would make a success of it. Children punished their parents by turning the tables and leaving home as soon as they could. But of course to punish your parents – not to love them – was the most violent and hideous of crimes; anyone guilty of that was thoroughly rotten and deserved destruction. As for all the conscientiousness, the perfectionism, it was an effort not to be interrogated, not to have one's real motives found out and exposed.

I have skimmed over this too quickly to be convincing, I fear, but the disentangling took some time – to realize that everyone's motives, including my own, had been far better than I thought. As I discovered this, and pieced together the misunderstandings and fumbled intentions and heartbreaks, and forgave others and myself, it was a religious experience, for at last I experienced the forgiveness of sins and the love of God. It brought to life what I was hearing at the Quaker meetings which I had started to attend. Up to then, Christianity had only spoken to me of total depravity and guilt: every crucified Christ reproached me: 'You did this to me.'

One of the hardest things about all this for my nearest and dearest was that I had not been able to tell them about my inner suffering. They had clues that something was wrong – outbursts of temper, the obsession with punctuality, sometimes a look of unspeakable sorrow on my face. It came as a terrible shock to them to hear that I had contemplated killing myself.

But most depressives cannot discuss their sensations with others. They know they will be assured that they are happy and successful and that their fears are nonsense. To have one's innermost knowledge of oneself dismissed like that is more than one can bear: it would be a kind of annihilation, to be told you are not the kind of person you know you are. You know you are so rotten that people will be better off without you; they will soon get over it. Your success in deceiving people only proves how rotten you are.

Well, it has gone now and I am content and happy, and accept my talents and my success. I do not want to kill myself, but if I were to be summoned tonight, I would go in peace.

And yet I have to be careful – twinges of that old panic and pursuit can still be brought on by overwork, for example. I try to avoid too much hurrying, to leave plenty of time for things. I think recovered depressives have to avoid certain 'triggers' that set them off. Overwork and rushing about are two of mine. Also (I am afraid) too much talking about depression, and the company of active fellow-depressives.

Psychiatry certainly transformed my religious life. If you have a sick mind, I am afraid you will have a sick faith and it only makes matters worse. I think the guilt-ridden 'there is no health in us' form of Christianity is a wicked perversion which obscures the primacy of grace and forgiveness. But it is all too easy for the depressive to miss that. My theology now emphasizes the notion of Christ – even the Father – suffering with us, descending into the darkness, and very positively rising again.

To be as practical as I can: how can we recognize depression in ourselves and in people close to us? Well, in my experience, there is suppressed violence at the heart of it, so there are outbursts of disproportionate rage. Bad sleeping: waking in the small hours and only falling asleep again when it is time to get up. Oddly enough, constipation. Sometimes a half-effort to say 'something is wrong with me'; and then you give up, because it will not be understood. Never say 'Oh, pull yourself together', because the sufferer cannot do so: he or she can only put on their disguise again and stagger on, flying on automatic pilot.

Very often there is a hereditary element in the illness: I can see now very clearly that it lay in my mother too. I think one is probably born with the tendency and circumstances may or may not develop it. In my case the 'talking treatment' worked, but I believe this is comparatively rare. Pills, the chemical treatment, are remarkably effective, although sufferers often resist them. I always say 'Take them – they are not to be despised, thousands of people owe their life and health to them'.

Then I have known electro-shock treatment to succeed (and from my observation it is by no means the horror people used to think). I have known diets to be effective, for in some cases an allergy seems to be involved. I know of four or five cases where the cattle-communicated disease brucellosis was involved and may have been the chemical trigger. So you see there is a family of diseases here, some internally and, some externally triggered (endogenous and exogenous, as they say) and a variety of possible treatments.

It has to be said that doctors vary in their competence at sorting all this out, and sometimes cases are mishandled or not taken seriously enough; but they are getting steadily better at it. The important thing is for depressives and their families to break the barrier of silence, to recognize that here is a treatable illness from which there can be recovery, not a madness, let alone a damnable sin that cannot be forgiven.

Talk delivered to the Romney Street Group on 3 March 1987.

13
The weakness of God

Today is Passion Sunday, the beginning of those two weeks in which the Church narrows its attention upon the most astonishing and often forgotten aspect of the Christian faith: the suffering of God – God's weakness.

But surely God is almighty, omnipotent, able to work any miracle he pleases? How can he be weak, vulnerable, suffering? It seems to me that unless we can explain this, our faith is in vain and we cannot tackle the main demand of the secular world today, which is to show, quite simply, that God exists. I say show, not prove, because anyone who expects the existence of God to be demonstrated by logic is playing at the wrong table. If it were possible to prove God logically, we would all have to become his slaves, which is not what a loving Father wants.

Those of us who know God – and none of us, even the most spiritual, has more than glimpsed his feet – know that God is indeed love. We know that, fundamentally, the universe is on our side; that it is permeated with a spirit that wills us to work with it, not against it, and a spirit that cares deeply and personally about us. I say that it grieves deeply and personally when we reject that will, that caring; and I say, too, that this is the central feature of the cross – the point at which God and man do cross, where God becomes man and says: 'I am like this: I have become you, and like you I am weak and I suffer.'

God weak? How can that be? We hear again the protest of the secular world 'I thought your God was omnipotent! What's all that stuff in the Old Testament about creating the heavens and the earth?' As indeed he did. But let us look more closely, and we shall see that from the beginning, from the very first appearance of man, God surrenders power and becomes weak, with that selfsame weakness that leads to the cross.

I am not proposing that we treat Genesis as a zoological textbook; that is to belittle it. It is something much more durable and metaphysical. The story of the choice of Adam and Eve to disobey God and help themselves to the power of moral decision symbolizes his gift to us of free will. All our decisions could have been made for us. We could have been 'programmed' to do nothing but the best, to be nothing but God's puppets. He could have made us so entirely obedient to his will that we never conflicted with one another, never took risks, never ran into any kind of danger. But if you reflect upon that, you will find that I am saying that he could have made us not to be men and women at all. And he could have made us so completely aware of his will that, while we might have feared him, we could never have loved him of our free choice. Love, to be love, cannot be coerced: it must be freely given, and that has to bring with it the freedom to withhold and to reject.

God, then, has weakened himself in giving us, like Adam and Eve, the freedom to reject him; and he is powerless if we choose to do so. God can only be active in human affairs with our co-operation, with the concurrence of our love and his; for as we ourselves know very well, from our own experience, love that is not recognized, responded to and worked with is love incomplete and frustrated.

God has also weakened himself by constructing not an arbitrary universe which he manipulates at whim, but a universe of natural laws which he himself must observe. A universe of perpetual miracles would be a universe of chaos in which any freedom of choice on our part would be pointless. And so he, too, loving his children, must suffer at the sight of earthquakes, famines, disease; longing, I am sure, that we would learn to understand these things better and handle them more wisely.

And so it came about that God's own Son – the ultimate sign of his love for us – was despised and rejected of men and nailed upon the cross by man's free will. And God was so weak that, his love being rejected, he could do nothing but hang there saying: 'I am like this: I am very like you.' He could do nothing but forgive – which is love, a form of love totally undeserved by those upon whom it is bestowed. Recognized, accepted and returned, it then becomes (as it has become) the mightiest power in the world: comforting, healing, pacifying, resurrecting – for never must we say the word crucifixion without resurrection. But first, the weakness of God, and then his power.

This short typescript was found among the author's papers after his death; it is undated.

14
The Trinity

The Trinity is a subject which I am usually inclined to squeeze past rather like a bulky piece of antique furniture, left by an aunt, but serving no useful purpose to the household today. Which of us really *uses* the Trinity today?

And yet we can hardly ignore it. It runs through the liturgy of the Church like a refrain – this continual three-fold rhythm 'In the name of the Father, and of the Son, and of the Holy Ghost' – and it is solemnly affirmed in the Creeds: the Father incomprehensible, the Son incomprehensible, the Holy Spirit incomprehensible, yet not three incomprehensibles but one incomprehensible. And we know that the Creeds were hammered out by the greatest minds of their day to preserve the faith against the onslaughts of heresy. They may mystify us, but they were vital to the early Church which stood so much closer to the Apostles and their Master than we ever can.

Yet where is the Trinity in the gospel? Some say it was present at the Baptism of Christ: Jesus himself, the voice of his Father, and the Dove descending. But we cannot see it very clearly in the Jesus manifesto: 'Repent, the kingdom of heaven is at hand, love one another, heal the sick' – and where is the Trinity in the Sermon on the Mount, or in the last discourse of St John? If it is so important, why is it not there?

True, it is there at the end of St Matthew: go and baptize in the name of the Father, Son and Holy Spirit. But this 'last minute appearance' makes it hard to see as an intrinsic part of Jesus' teaching. We cannot help suspecting that it was inserted by a zealous Trinitarian some time later.

It is possible to argue ingeniously that the Trinity is implied in two or three passages in St Paul. But it is far from being explicit or essential: the grounds are really not much better than they are for the cult of the Virgin. We may subscribe to the doctrine of the Trinity because we are told the Church requires it, but is it really as personally convincing? I find, incidentally, that some Christians are essentially worshippers of the Father, some of the Son, others of the Holy Spirit – but very few of the Trinity.

I think we can see how the Trinity arose naturally and inevitably from the experience of the Apostles – an experience which we cannot ourselves reproduce. As Jews rooted in Jewish history they were convinced of God the Father – the one God, no other gods but he. But they had known Jesus, and whatever they had thought him to be at first, they came to see him as divine – perhaps not the whole of God (how could he be, since he spoke to a Father outside and above himself?) but wholly God. Jesus had been taken from the disciples; yet they had become filled with yet another divine experience which Jesus had promised them – the Holy Spirit. Three persons, all different yet all of God – the Trinity.

Yet they were Jews – monotheists – and as they sought to explain their experience they had to tell their fellow Jews 'God is more than the Father', and they had to tell the pagans 'God is not your *Gods* – he is One'. So we arrive eventually at the paradox of the Creeds. And paradox about God is fair enough: if there is a God, he must be beyond our ability to define. Yet, if he loves us and reaches down to us, he will surely offer some image of himself that we can grasp.

Jews and Muslims cannot be persuaded that the Trinity is not a cover-up for a limited polytheism. Jews, in particular, cannot be persuaded that Jesus himself could have claimed divinity – let alone walked the earth saying 'I am the Second Person of the Trinity'. Personally I do not think that he did. I think he may have expected everyone to sense the Fatherhood of God in the way he did, and have come to realize with horror that his intimacy with the Father was unique – was not shared by his followers. Towards the end, though, in Gethsemane, we hear him submitting to a will that was not wholly his own . . .

I have come to realize that doctrines like the Trinity are not and cannot be complete descriptions of God. They are better than nothing for our purposes; they are signposts pointing a direction, and not the destination itself. What the doctrine of the Trinity indicates to me is that God is not a static monolith, but a system of relationships within which there is constant activity. God is not just 'up there' in heaven, or even around us outside in the universe; he is also 'in here', in all of us, incarnated in man ('yet not I, but Christ in me'). And the two are not cut off from each other. The Father (the God without) communicates with the Son (the God within) and the two-way flow between them is the Holy Spirit.

A scientist with whom I discussed this pointed out that the Trinity is a model of modern communications theory. The minimum conditions for communication are two points or poles and the flow between them. And note something further that arises.

Many unchurched believers still imagine that our religion is really a kind of respectable magic: that we feel uneasy about the mysterious force above us, so we send up smoke signals and other magic spells to manipulate and appease that force. But this is what Christianity is about; it tells us that God is not just out there, he is also in here, and our communication with him is two-way. He actually starts the relationship, and we respond. He, the Father, sends down the Spirit to the Son within us, and the Son responds. Thus the Trinity is the condition for Christian worship – which is essentially a matter of message and response, or as some would say, communion.

This short manuscript was found among the author's papers after his death; it cannot be dated with precision, but clearly precedes his stroke in June 1989.

15
What it is not

As a listener, I usually have to spend the first five minutes of any address picking out the code-words being used and calculating where the speaker is speaking from. 'Ah!' (I say to myself) 'Conservative Evangelical with a touch of Calvinism . . .', or 'Catholic Liberationist with a guilty conscience about feminism. . .'

I do not know how well-informed you are about such theological codes, so I will try to save you trouble by telling you where I think I stand – or at least have stood: for I should hate to think that like one of those mobile homes that has lost its wheels, I was no longer on the move.

I was brought up, then, middle-of-the-road Anglican, King James Bible and the Book of Common Prayer; indulgent towards the Methodists because they had so many good hymns, prejudiced against the Catholics because the Pope was not British and you had to be Irish to join anyway.

At the age of eighteen I got fed up with the Anglicans – their vain repetitions, their flabby sermons and priest-dominated congregations – so I joined the English Presbyterians where the preaching was more aggressive; anyway, it was in the tradition of my mother's family which was Scottish. And I stayed in the United Reformed tradition of the Presbyterians and Congregationalists until two things happened to me simultaneously – I got pacifism (largely as a result of working as a reporter in Vietnam and the American ghetto riots of the 1960s) and it began to dawn on me that instead of telling God who he was and what he ought to be doing for us (which presumably he knew already) it might be a good idea to shut up and listen in case *he* had something to say. In short, I joined the Society of Friends (the Quakers), who in this country are almost entirely of the unstructured, contemplative variety, theologically liberal and with no professional ministry.

It has be admitted that there are not many of us in Britain – less than 20,000 – but we seem to enjoy a respect and influence out of proportion to our numbers (whether we deserve that respect and influence is another matter).

Personally I see us as a lay society within the great Church of the followers of Jesus: I do not approve of Quaker isolationism, and though I tease the clergy a good deal I am not anti-clerical; some of my best friends are deans and bishops. The sacraments have never played a big part in my religious life, though I accept them when it seems appropriate and does not give offence. I preach a fair amount from a variety of pulpits, and because I still find the mainstream theological vocabulary useful for such purposes, I am afraid some of my fellow Quakers regard me as an Anglican Entryist; many Anglicans, on the other hand, regard me as a heretic. 'Freelance part-time amateur theologian' might perhaps describe me best; although, curiously, I find I get on very well with the Catholics and Orthodox, because for all their dogmas and sacraments there comes a point when they and the Quakers do share together the riches of silence – of confessing that God is *not* this, *not* that, *not* the other, and that all we can do in the end is trust the incomprehensible.

That is why I have called this talk 'What it is not' – 'it' being our religion as I see it. In a poor way I am hobbling after such spiritual giants as Basil the Great and Gregory of Nyssa, as well as the author of *The Cloud of Unknowing*, which is Holy Scripture to many English Quakers. Like Pseudo-Dionysius, I think the cataphatic theological games we play (saying God *is* this, that and the other), while they do provide us with some useful knowledge of God, are only provisional, metaphorical, corrigible, open-ended; they are mere preludes to the apophatic surrender.

In that case, why say anything? Because we must. We are made that way; and I think we are made to shed our illusions by examining them and testing them – climbing up and up, using and discarding this concept and then that, as the air gets rarer and clearer towards the summit. Have no fear, though, that I shall leave you with nothing to believe at all. We are not going to get to the summit – not in this lifetime – and those of us who must live in the world, who cannot afford a cave in the desert, will have to go on saying (provisionally) that God *is* 'whatever'. For if we are to handle those fragments of the truth we can cope with – if we are to pick them up from the past, handle them in the present and pass them on to the future – they have to be packaged and labelled. I say they are fragments of the truth: they are models of it, pointers to it, guesses at it. They are not the truth. For the truth itself is somewhere else: it is *not* this, it is *not* that, though it may have had some connection with it. God would not be the God that he is if we could prove that he was; and the day we can put God in a box, the world will come to an end.

Now I suppose that was an apophatic prelude to a cataphatic disquisition. Because I am bound to try and say something positive, even if it does not amount to very much; and while I hope to dismiss two or three illusions as to what our religion is about, you will have reason to be disappointed if I do not leave you with some suggestions that may endure a while. So I think we must get it clear that our religion is not about magic; that it is not about success; that it is not about being good. I think it is about making sense of the will of God, which is the love of God. In a word, it is about grace; and the more we come to realize that, the less we can do anything but adore it.

I think it is rather important that our religion should be useless, in the sense that it should not be something we can employ for our own advantage. At the heart of it, it must be something we do because we can do no other: something that leaves the irreligious gasping 'But why on earth do that? It accomplishes nothing!'

'I should hope not!' is the answer. 'Anyone can accomplish things. I am doing this for the love of God.'

Now at this point someone ought to remind me that the Christian gospel does very much enjoin us to accomplish things. We are commanded (as we shall answer at the dreadful day of judgement) to feed the hungry, clothe the naked, visit the sick and imprisoned, and we are shown that doing it for them is doing it for God himself. But, as I read the parable, anyone can do these good deeds without being consciously a Christian. All around us today we can see non-Christians performing good works whose merits is surely not diminished thereby. We are making a terrible mistake if we imagine that only

Christians do famine relief or hospice nursing, and a worse mistake still if we imagine that God discounts the good works of the heathen.

I am actually talking about spiritual activities – about worship, prayer, meditation, ministry of the word and – even – of the sacraments. For I do see some danger in our churches of confusing the religious imperative with other imperatives. A church is not simply a praying-machine; but it is not a social welfare organization, nor is it an investment trust, nor an arts club, nor a political party. I am emphatically not saying that the Church should keep out of politics or art or social welfare, but it must remember that these are not primarily what it is for; it is not necessarily going to be very good at these activities, it should not pretend to know a detailed Christian way of going about them, and I think that Christians should be pretty loose to party loyalties and unreliable as party hacks.

Before we pretend to show God, we must know God. Before we breathe out, we must breathe in. Before we presume to say 'Thus saith the Lord', we must be silent and hear him; and we had better to be very sure we have heard him aright, or else remain silent. There is not enough listening today. We are too ready to pick up a fragment of a rumour of what God has said and run through the streets with it crying 'Behold the will of God! It's exactly what we wanted!' That may be so; but is it what he wants? What makes us so sure that he has a policy on the matter?

As you may know, Quaker business meetings are conducted in a spirit of worship. We do not take any votes. In theory at least, when we meet to decide what colour to paint the meeting house door we are not interested in determining how many members would like it red, green or blue; we endeavour to arrive at a consensus – although the pious fiction is that we are trying to ascertain the will of the Spirit, which probably turns out to be an inoffensive grey.

Now, that may in fact be the colour which offends the fewest members and therefore creates the least ill-feeling, and there is a great deal to be said for that. But it does not follow that grey is aesthetically best; and as for the Spirit, I do not think he (or she) gives a damn. Transporting this to the political arena, I am not sure the Spirit cares whether the hospital service is socialized or privatized, so long as the sick are cared for according to their needs. I think that if we stop putting words into God's mouth (and that includes borrowing them out of context from the Bible) we shall find him far less talkative and yet far more demanding of our own thought and effort than we suppose. Beware of the Bible! It is a very holy book – or rather, a library of books – but it is not a work of divination, like the Chinese I-Ching, nor a collection of spells, and it needs to be handled with the greatest of care and with fastidious scholarship.

In particular, we have to remind ourselves of the danger of reading our own attitudes back into it, in ways that may be out of context, inappropriate and wholly unintended by the authors. That we can do so is one of the things that makes it such a marvellous work; but is it really the Spirit shining forth from a certain passage, or merely our own wish fulfilment? That is one reason why I respect the traditional Church, for all its failings: we would not have the Bible at all without the Church, and it is wrong to elevate the Scriptures above the Church as if they had an independent existence.

Now I have said that religion is not magic; and this is part of what I meant. But vast numbers of ordinary people still regard the operations of the Churches as an attempt to manipulate God with spells and rituals, and to figure out the coded messages he is thought to have hidden away in the Bible. It is as if worship were a series of smoke-signals we sent up in the hope that there was Somebody above the clouds who might notice them and respond favourably. Say the right words in the right order and he will send the rains, prosper the crops and preserve an otherwise doomed marriage. Many of us would like to believe that – and did not Jesus tell us that whatsoever we asked for in his name would be granted us? And I know people who have prayed for jobs, exam results, sums of money, and got them; one young lady even told me she had prayed for a new car and got it! 'But isn't that the car that kept getting into accidents?' I reminded here. 'Ah', she said, 'that was the Devil.'

All this is sheer mumbo-jumbo and not the God I know. Quite apart from the Devil (who seems to have taken early retirement and left us to do his work for him), do we really believe in a God who can be wheedled and cajoled, who has to be told how great and good he is before he will distribute the candy? Believe me, flattery will get you nowhere with God; nor is he going to run around the universe making nonsense of it by granting special exceptions to a few who get the words right.

Which is not to say that I do not believe in prayer. For a start, I believe in its discipline: I think it is good for us to confess our dependence upon God, to give thanks, to complain perhaps, and to adore; but when it comes to our petitions I do not think we should adopt an attitude of 'Give me' or even 'Please give me' or 'Please give my friend'. Jesus' petitions were often not granted. Nevertheless, 'Thy will be done' was a way of coming to terms with and learning to accept the superior wisdom. So I think that when we have a petition to make, rather than pressing it upon God with our urgent recommendation for action, we should hold our need or our hurt up to him and then attend patiently for what he will make of it. We need to be open, honest and attentive; not ambitious, self-excusing and full of helpful suggestions.

I believe in the conversation between God and humankind. But it goes on all the time. Our worship is not a magic ceremony to rouse the slumbering deity and get him to dance to our tune; it is our dance to his tune, our response to the grace he pours down upon us; for grace is like electricity, in that the circuit has to be completed before it can flow and energize. Until we recognize grace for what it is and respond to it, it is grace frustrated; so, if you like, it is God who is trying to work the magic spell of getting us to respond, not we him. And instead of searching the Bible for secrets about his past, we should concentrate on the new Bible which he calls upon us daily to act out; for is not the story of his people a continuing one?

And yet the Bible makes abundantly clear that our religion is not about success, for at the historical level it records a series of appalling failures, with the crucifixion and the destruction of Jerusalem as its apparent climax. The Protestant Ethic has tended to dwell at times on the rewards lavished by God on his elect, but I do not think many of us who contemplate the Third World or the nuclear arms race would be able to rest for long on that comfort. Here in Britain we see success in decline, having been lucky to escape the material destruction that was visited on our opponents forty years ago. Meanwhile the world's poor people rot and starve, regardless of whether they are Christians in Brazil or pagans in the Sudan. And whether we take the view that they are feckless (as the Victorians did of the starving Irish) or are being punished by God for attending the wrong church, or we conclude that there is no God at all, it is quite clear that there is no correlation at all between churchgoing (however devout) and prosperity. It was, I think, the English scientist Galton who sought to demonstrate statistically that prayer was ineffective: nobody, he argued, was more systematically prayed for than the royal families of the world, and yet no class was more liable to assassination; therefore prayer was ineffective. What I think that really shows is that Galton misunderstood the nature of prayer, and perhaps he was not the only one.

Then, of course, the rich and successful can be miserable, too, and often are. They suffer from depression, get betrayed by their partners, have their children take to drugs and themselves to drink; they are just as liable to be spiritually dead, if not more so than the rest of us, and I think that Jesus appreciated this. I do not think he ever joined the class war against the rich, for he always judged people on their own merits and their honesty; he just knew, sadly, that the material entanglements of the successful made it almost impossible for them to spend time on the things of the spirit.

Does that mean that the poor are morally and spiritually superior? I do not think this is true to experience, since poverty can be hideously corrupting, nor do I think it was what Jesus meant. I think he really was promising them pie in the sky, or, rather, in the Kingdom that was coming; and he may well be right, we shall see. At the same time, he was all for improving the lot of the unfortunate here and now. He did not, however, tell them to 'Follow me and get rich quick'. For one thing, I believe he thought the end of the world was at hand and getting rich hardly mattered. One of our problems – one of the great problems of the Church – is that the end did not happen and, from being an abject failure, our religion became a great success with power and money and property piling up. But that is not what it was about, ever. I doubt, however, whether the answer is for the churches literally to sell all they have and give to the poor; we live in a thoroughly compromised world, with a compromised Church. What would happen if the Church did just dissolve itself and disperse its funds? What witness would there be left? I am afraid that within a few months such potential as it had to do good works would have vanished into the sand, and its members would be left at the mercy of the godless religions of secularism.

Some people think our religion is about being good. When I was little I was taught to pray 'And make me a good boy – Amen.' Well, he did not do it, and you persistently hear the complaint that 'Church people are a lot of hypocrites, they are no better than anyone else', followed by the story of how one of the local elders beats his wife.

No one holds firmer views of what it is like in church than those who do not go – which is why they do not go. Personally I think churchgoers tend to be a bit nicer than other people – maybe I just find them my sort of folk – but I do know they go to church because they admit their hypocrisy, because they know they are sinners, because they confess it and seek forgiveness, which is always poured out and waiting for us if only we will acknowledge our need of it, reach out and take it.

Now, I have no patience with people who say that if there is a God, he must be a monster because surely we deserve something a great deal better than we get. Surely the baby dying of starvation, the mother in agony from cancer, the young man crushed in an earthquake, all deserve something better? But the fact is that we deserve nothing, and it is amazing what we do get even so. Unless this really is a world where success is attainable by magic, we are faced with the truth that we do not *earn* a life of rewards and punishments from God. That was always a fallacy and it holds no water at all today. I cannot expound a whole theodicy now; much of our suffering is our own fault, not God's; some of it is the unavoidable consequence of living in the only possible universe which could have produced *us* (and yet we complain that it is not good enough); there is a price to pay for it all, and I believe that God pays in suffering even more, and that is what the cross is all about. What I am trying to say is that our religion is not about rewards for the righteous, but is actually much more about why bad things happen to good people.

As a Quaker – and a recovered depressive – I have to confess that I am not terribly interested in sin and guilt, and I reject total depravity, though I do not go as far as George Fox who was thrown into jail for claiming to be 'a man free from sin' and assailed the Puritan preachers who (he said) were constantly 'roaring up for sin'. We *are* sinful, even the best of us, but I think it is blasphemous to claim that we are made in the image of God and, at the same time, that 'there is no health in us'. Of course there is health in us, for the Holy Spirit is in us, as it is in every man, woman and child, though often neglected and obscured. Conversion (when it happens) is not a matter of injecting something from outside, but is the arousal of something that is already there.

The important thing about morality – and the reason why I say it is not what our religion is about – is that it is natural, rational and human. It is living in accordance with our true nature (something we make very difficult for ourselves by devising ways of life that are exceedingly unnatural and more complicated than we can cope with). You do not have to be a Christian or Jew to be a virtuous and charitable citizen. Values like honesty, courage, kindness, service and fidelity are acknowledged worldwide. What the British like to think of as 'the Christian virtues' are largely those of the classical Stoics, while the Ten Commandments are essentially the social rules of the club – a sensible way of preserving law and order in the tribe. It does not surprise me that God should give such commandments his blessing, because he wills our welfare and not our downfall; nor is it surprising that things go wrong when we ignore them. Different cultures will stress different virtues according to their circumstances; but by and large there is nothing mystical about morality. What is right is usually quite sensible; difficulties and dilemmas set in where two or more issues collide and we find ourselves having to choose the better of two 'not-so-goods', to the prejudice of the other. But it is no easier, I think, for the Christian to make such choices than it is for the atheist; and there are plenty of morally upright unbelievers.

I am not, of course, advocating antinomianism – not maintaining that moral law is not binding on Christians, like the seventeenth-century Ranters who claimed that Christ had abolished sin and the whole of creation was there to be enjoyed without inhibition. But morality is not a Christian monopoly and little, if any, of it is dictated by exclusively Christian concerns. If there is one peculiarly Christian contribution to morality – and I have to say it is not a popular one: it is ill thought of by practical men of the world – it is to be found on the cross, in redemptive suffering, unrequited concession, turning the other cheek. I would argue that it is, in fact, practical – for the greatest good of the greatest number, even – but you have only to consider how pacifism is generally regarded to note that my view is not the world view.

In this question of the Christian moral imperative to suffer evil without hitting back, I think we reach the borderline or transition between my contention that our religion is *not* about being good and the commonsense claim that it *is*. It really is the key question, for my contention that suffering is practical is highly debatable. Would it have been practical *not* to resist Hitler? Or have we moved into the area of pure religion where the holy gesture has to be be made for its own sake and not for the sake of any result? I have to admit I am in an awkward position here, because I find it very difficult to accept the high metaphysical view of the crucifixion which sees it as a mystical sacrifice affecting the whole moral chemistry of the universe: that *he* died for *our* sins, which are ours, not his, and which we still commit regardless. I can see the cross as a sign of how God is, of what he is like and what he does by sharing in the mess which is our existence rather than standing aside from it. But the mess still goes on. Was it wrong to fight Hitler rather than be crucified by him? It is not in my heart to say it was wrong, any more than I could say it was wrong for society to resist a murderer, rapist or terrorist.

It seems to me that on the cross God is saying 'I am like this: this is how I am and always will be, whether you respond or not. You may fight evil in your own way, but this is the only way I can do it.' Some of us – the saints and martyrs – will feel called to imitate that example out of sheer love for him, but I see this as an act of worship, not of natural morality. It is not a question of being good but of being holy.

You will see that I am trying to head off claims that this or that policy is right because it is Christian. I hope Christians do right, because they should have a full view of what it is to be truly human. Sometimes they find this difficult because the churches have narrowed that view down, pinched bits of it out, saying 'You are not a child of God unless you are a born-again, adult-baptized, fundamentalist, vegetarian speaker-in-tongues!' – or maybe a pre-Vatican II celibate Catholic with a scourge under your pillow. Details like that are taking us back again to the world of magical religion, of attempting to earn our way to heaven by taking thought for it. That great spiritual director the Abbé de Tourville used to urge his clients to stop trying to imitate the saints and be what they were. 'When will you get it into your head', he used to write, 'that God loves you just as you are? Don't be proud of that; just be grateful and get on with your life.' He certainly did not think that religion was about being good; nor, I think, did Jesus, who notoriously consorted with drunks and sinners and detested people who thought themselves righteous. What appealed to him was self-honesty and a readiness to pick oneself up and start again.

Certainly our religion should help us to do that. But still I do not think that is the heart of the matter. What is? What is it about?

I say it is about making sense of the mess we are in, and we cannot do that by persuading it to go our way (because it will not) nor by mastering it (because we cannot) nor by scoring Brownie points (by which God is not impressed). We can only make sense by getting to know God, recognizing his will for us, which is that unearned love known as grace – when it is gratefully recognized, accepted and returned. This process can go on anywhere, all day long, as it does with saints who just live grace all the time. But most of us need special periods of concentration like prayer, meetings for worship, services and sacraments; it does require some discipline, which is why I am suspicious of laid-back do-it-yourself religion, walking in the forest or listening to string quartets.

I think our religion is about nothing less than the encounter with God himself, or at least with training ourselves for it; and when we do get close to him, then it is time to become speechless and adore and let him take over. Then, perhaps, we will actually find ourselves behaving better, loving and serving others better, finding a new meaning to success, realizing how our prayers are answered in unexpected ways. A sceptic might comment 'So everything is the same, really; it is just that you have decided to look at it through God-tinted glasses'. And the answer is 'No, everything is totally different. How can it be otherwise when you realize that the maker of the universe is in love with you, and you with him?'

This paper was originally delivered to the North American Summer School at Mansfield College, Oxford, in July 1986, and repeated before an audience at Damascus House, Mill Hill, London, the following November.

Facing Last Things

16
An unpopular sermon

This is the most unpopular sermon I know, and I will tell you how I came upon it.

Some years ago, my family and I were living in the United States, in a prosperous suburb of Washington. Churchgoing was the fashion (if not altogether the conviction) of my respectable neighbours; and every Sunday morning, just before eleven, there was the biggest traffic-jam of the week, as Catholics and Episcopalians, Baptists, Methodists and the rest, tried to park their station waggons as near as possible to the family place of worship.

In those days, before I realized the folly of sermon-preaching, I favoured attendance at the local Presbyterian church – one of the more up-market denominations in America. This particular congregation was booming. The building itself (know as 'the plant') included a Christmas-card-Gothic nave with a large crypt for the overflow, a large and a small hall, a suite of offices, and a row of classrooms for Sunday School. The clergy were organized along the lines of a cabinet, with a Minister for Worship, a Minister for Education, a Minister for Music and (with a degree in business studies) a Minister for Finance. There were also Assistant Ministers, and it was one of these – a radical who had slipped in like a mole somehow – who inspired what I now have to say.

It was not the custom in this church to disturb the faithful. Our sermons were like pullovers: warm, woolly and comfortable. The lawyers, civil servants and bankers did not wish to stand exposed to the icy blast of judgement and prophecy; but that is what happened one Sunday.

Our preacher began, routinely enough, by reading from Luke, chapter 12, beginning at verse 16. You will recall the rich man who built new barns to store his great wealth, saying

> Soul, thou hast much goods laid up for many years; take thine ease, eat, drink, and be merry. But God said unto him, Thou fool, this night thy soul shall be required of thee: then whose shall those things be, which thou hast provided? So is he that layeth up treasure for himself, and is not rich toward God.

(A better translation is really 'but is a pauper in the sight of God'.)

I find this parable crammed with meanings. But it so happened that our preacher in Washington that day chose to dwell upon the imminence and unpredictability of death. Standing upon this parable, he warned the lawyers and bankers that their career plans and investment schedules could be revoked in the twinkling of an eye by the dread words: 'Thou fool, this night thy soul shall be required of thee.'

It was not well received; and within a month, our assistant minister was called elsewhere. To my lasting regret, I never knew what became of him. But that text has remained with me ever since: 'Thou fool, this night thy soul shall be required of thee.' Those words stand as the possible context for everything we do. None of us can be certain that tomorrow's sunrise will be ours, or that we can afford to deviate briefly from what is right, on the grounds that we shall have plenty of time later to get back on course. We may not have – and that is part of the lesson of this parable.

But we should begin by considering the context of this story. Jesus has been talking about God's caring presence in the life of every individual. And then somebody barges in, assuming that, like any rabbi, Jesus cares as much about social law as he does about salvation. And he asks Jesus to act as arbitrator in a dispute about his late father's estate: 'Speak to my brother, that he divide the inheritance with me.'

Jesus declines. 'Who made me a judge or a divider over you?' One might interpret this politically, as showing that Jesus is not very much concerned with economic justice; but I fancy this is not a case of rich man versus poor man, but of two well-to-do people, neither of whom is in much real distress. Jesus can afford to say to them: Never mind your treasure; you have so much that you can even afford to build new warehouses for it. God is totally unimpressed: you cannot *buy* a better seat in heaven. But what about your immortal soul?

You will notice that the rich man in the parable really does think there is a nourishing connection between his money and his spirit. 'Soul', he says, 'thou hast much goods laid up . . . eat, drink, and be merry.' He really believes that wealth can give him a soft ride through life, and frankly, there is some truth in that. As God points out, you cannot take it with you; but while you have got it, it can be very reassuring. Jesus goes on to tell his disciples not to worry about food or drink or clothing, but to sell what they have and give alms to the poor and concentrate on the spiritual life. But I get the impression from the gospels as a whole that he does not reject the man of property as a class; he judges him according to how he deploys his wealth towards others.

Undoubtedly this parable is a warning to the rich that worldly success does not impress God. Money will not buy life, let alone salvation. But I do not think this parable would have such a haunting power if that were the whole significance of it.

I find it significant that the man himself addresses his 'soul', as, indeed, God does. So at a deeper level we can see the story as a warning to the man of the spirit, also, and not simply to the man of property. None of us should think that we have got it made because we have achieved something spiritually and intellectually: that because we have published a successful book or been appointed to a fellowship we can now lie back and rest on our laurels. I see this parable as a warning against the corruption of success in all fields: for the cleric, the academic and the businessman alike can all be successful in the eyes of the world, and a pauper in the eyes of God. And this night their souls may be required of them, and God will judge them by his standards, not theirs. What his standards are is what the gospels are really about.

I come back, though, to the most obvious message of the parable, the one that shocked my fellow Presbyterians so deeply that they sacked the messenger that brought them the bad news – the news that we are all condemned to death, and that everything we do has to be seen in the context of our approaching end.

Whatever we believe about life after death, it is not news to be taken lightly. It tells the ambitious careerist that it is no use pinning his hopes upon plans that will take years to mature: he may not have those years. The warning of mortality is put with greater optimism in the verses that follow, where Jesus tells his disciples not to worry about living; God will take care of that, as he will take care of how we are to die. It may sound cold comfort (though when you have contemplated it for some time it becomes reassuring) but the fact is, we need not concern ourselves about the manner of our death: God will take care of that for us.

Jesus himself, even before the resurrection, had no doubt that there is a life after death. But he did not attempt, nor does the Church, to describe that life; it could not possibly be understood in the terms of this world. Some Christians, rather than declaring 'I believe in God', prefer in all honesty to say more simply 'I trust God'. Belief might seem to imply a certainty that comes from knowing and checking, which we do not presume to claim. But trust is something we can confirm by experience, by putting ourselves into God's hands and seeing what happens.

This is the kind of experience that enabled St Francis of Sales to urge: 'Do not fear what may happen tomorrow. The same everlasting Father who cares for you today will take care of you then and every day. He will either shield you from suffering or give you unfailing strength to bear it. Be at peace, and put aside all anxious thoughts and imaginations.'

Easier said than done, perhaps. But until we can do it, death will remain a source of bitterness and fear. And this is largely because we are too selfish about life – our own life and that of others. After all, we are not entitled to live forever, or even to secure whatever length of life and style of death we think we deserve. God does not hand out long life and easy death to the good, short life and torment to the wicked. Jesus' own death shows us that life span is not awarded as a prize for godliness. Some would argue that this proves there is no God, only a series of brutal accidents; but that is not the experience of those who have trusted God over the centuries. Part of their answer must be that unless we are to be purely God's puppets (which would rule out any real love between us and him) we are bound to run the risk of suffering.

So the Christian has to be prepared, without anxiety, for death at any moment. And, paradoxically, a soul which accepts that and is ready for death is perfectly prepared for life as well, valuing every moment of it as a unique blessing. We are all under suspended sentence of death, from the moment of our conception. We have done nothing to earn or deserve being born at all. Every day of life is a privilege extended to us by the grace of God.

Fine talk, but how, in the end, can we face death? The hardest part is 'letting go', both of our own life and of those we (sometimes selfishly) love. We can best do both by realizing that, under God, neither our own life nor that of others is our private property. Death can come easier if we can see ourselves as part of a continuity – best of all, of a family. In a sense, we have to move on so that others can take our place. If we are lucky enough to have a family, we should do everything in our power to love it, keep it in good repair, and pass on to it those things we have found in life that may be of use to it. But we should not make the mistake of loving too narrowly. Christians must love their neighbours and their friends, not just their husband or wife or children. Spreading our love makes it go further in the end.

No one should pretend that death, when it comes, can be trimmed of all bitterness, or that it is wrong to break down and weep when a loved one is called away. We are right to grieve spontaneously, and I have been told that it takes most people about two years to recover fully from a close bereavement. A church funeral can play a very important part in this process: it is designed for the benefit of the living, rather than the dead, for it makes us come to terms with the facts, gives us a chance to say farewell, to give thanks for the life which is past, purge ourselves of regret, and show respect without haste or impersonality.

Finally, let me say something about death from my own experience. Looking on both my parents within an hour or two of their deaths, I had the overwhelming impression not that they were dead, but that they were not there, they had gone somewhere else. And on the two occasions when my own life was in crisis, there was no fear. One felt the systems of the body 'switching off' one by one, leaving one with no more than one could cope with. In my case, they came back on again. But like most people who have been up to the brink in this way, the experience left me with no anxieties about my end today.

I began this address with the ominous words: 'This night thy soul shall be required of thee.' Let me end it by repeating some others: 'The same everlasting Father who cares for you today will take care of you every day. He will either shield you from suffering or give you unfailing strength to bear it. Be at peace . . .'

Sermon preached in Wesley Church, Oxford, on 23 October 1983.

17

Life after death

Some years ago, when I was doing a 'Your religious questions answered' programme on Radio 2, the commonest query I received was from distraught ladies anxiously enquiring 'Has my budgie gone to heaven?' That may sound silly in public; but I can assure you that privately it meant an awful lot to those asking it, who were dear, good, caring people in need of comfort. So I had to refrain from telling them to love people rather than birds; and that no church has ever credited animals with immortal souls. Instead I had to evolve a soothing rigmarole about how, since Budgie has become a part of your heart, I am sure you will take him with you wherever you go in this world or the next. This is what is known as a pious fraud, and theologically I felt very uncomfortable with it. But if ever I reach the groves of paradise, I shall have this academic interest in seeing whether I am greeted by flocks of beatified budgies.

But life after death for humans? Is it true? And what can it be? Must a Christian believe in it here and now? Apparently so: for we are required to affirm 'the resurrection of the body and the life everlasting. Amen.' Obviously this goes back to the Christian insistence that Jesus rose from the dead – was not defeated by death – though, as my good friend the Bishop of Durham observes (and St Paul supports him), it was not just a conjuring trick with bones. The risen Christ was something other than that, and something much more. In any case he told his disciples that he was not yet ascended, that what they saw was not yet completed.

The resurrection of Jesus tells us that death has been conquered, but it does not tell us exactly how. It is inconceivable to me that the Christian faith could have endured its first three centuries of scorn and persecution if nothing had really happened after the crucifixion. But what happened was surely unique: the empty tomb is not a performance that God obligingly repeats before our eyes to demonstrate objectively that it will necessarily happen to us in just the same way.

Logically, life after death is nonsense. To be alive is to be not dead; to be dead is to be not alive: you cannot be both at once. So if our subject has any meaning at all, as I think it has, then, to extend the paradox, we are talking about a condition in which we are conscious of being ourselves yet without bodily senses, a condition of which we have no experience at all (so far), and without experience, anything we say must sound like guesswork. I am sorry if I offend those who will say 'but the Bible promises it'. The Bible cannot be true simply because it says it is true; that is a disreputable proposition. The very word 'true' can mean many different things. I think the Bible is not misleading; but it is not to be read as if it were a reference manual or a history book.

You and I are human beings. We each have a body which we can see and feel and measure and photograph – something material and distinct. No two are quite the same. We also have a history of consciousness, tightly linked with that body, which is equally distinct but not material. And on the face of things it does not seem possible that this consciousness – this awareness of ourselves and others which we can turn over and examine backwards and forwards – could continue without the bodily equipment that enables us to see and feel and measure. We know that when somebody dies (whatever that means) the body decays and then disperses, leaving nothing to distinguish you from me as we are now. What 'life' could there be then? Only a life that is not what we mean by life as we now live it.

And yet I do believe in some kind of life after death. For the moment I will give you just one simple and inadequate reason. When I saw my father and later my mother lying dead, it was not at all like seeing them asleep. Nor was I looking at machines which had broken down and come irreparably to a halt. The overwhelming impression I had was that *they were not there*; they were somewhere else; they had transferred, and I am not able to doubt that.

Of course there is an element of wishful thinking. I should like to believe that the death of my body and the bodies of those I love is not the end. It would seem a waste, an absurdity, to have come so far only to shut down the show. And if you believe in a loving God – which perhaps is the heart of the matter – it just does not seem like him to behave absurdly.

I do not think we can discuss the matter without also taking into account the fact that a belief in life after death goes back a very long way into the human past. Indeed, the principle seems to have been taken for granted for many thousands of years. What we might crudely call 'the cave-man' looked on the face of the dead and decided the real person had gone elsewhere. So in many civilizations we find the corpse buried with food and possessions for use in that other world – even slaughtered servants and bodyguards for the nobility – and we find, too, agreement on a long journey underground through various obstacles and ordeals to a final judgement and (hopefully) a land of bliss based on the more desirable features of the life we know. Egyptian tomb-paintings depict this journey methodically; they are veritable prompt-books of the answers the spirit must give to its various interrogators. We find something similar in the Graeco-Roman myths about crossing the river to the Elysian Fields. The details of our belief have varied, but the principle seems to be part of the condition of being human. Like our apprehension of God, it is part of the equipment which has enabled us to come so far along the evolutionary path. In that sense we can say 'It works' and therefore is not to be lightly cast aside.

You may feel inclined to reply that the validity of magic was equally accepted for almost as long, but has been abandoned by most of us as science has revealed how things really work. The old belief in immortality rested on the assumption that body and soul were separate entities. There is a possible exception in some ancestor cults, which you could say were precursors of the modern idea that we 'live on' in our children and grandchildren; but I do not really think that this is what Christians are talking about – even if scientifically it seems more plausible and might also appeal to reincarnationists. The point is, now that science has revealed how the human organism functions, and that there is no 'detachability' between body and soul, such that one could exist without the other, should we not also abandon the magical believe in survival after death?

For a start, I cannot understand why the discoveries of science should ever have been seen as disproving the existence of God and of the spiritual dimensions. They certainly proved the clumsiness of humankind's earlier attempts to analyse nature; but science is constantly proving, too, the temporary and provisional character of its own analysis, which in turn is revealing the ingenuity and glory of creation as a continuing process. I really do not see why God should be diminished when his works are shown to be technologically so brilliant and (in a word) scientific. An arbitrary God would be a monster, as indeed he often seemed to be in the past.

But neither do I see how scientific and technological analysis can add up to the human personality. X pounds of protein, Y pints of water, several ounces of this, that and the other chemical plus a few volts of electricity, however ingeniously arranged, do not give you Mother Teresa or even Harold Fosdyke – they just do not add up. The oddest thing of all, perhaps, is that the whole formula is able to look at itself, as it were from outside itself, and engage in the sort of speculation that we are engaged in now. How can this be, if there is nothing that can (so to speak) 'take off and look down'?

It even seems to me that there is in fact some sort of magic – though that is a word to make the clergy shudder; they would probably prefer spiritual or divine power, or maybe grace – anyway, some influence not dependent upon the body – and I encounter it in prayer. This is not the place for a dissertation upon prayer; but if you have ever been prayed for you may know what I mean. I am not saying that this proves life after death, but it does tell me there is something in us that can be active without bodily presence.

It may be relevant to mention here, in passing, the theory of Pascal's Best Bet. The French theologian argued that the wise man should put his faith in life after death, because if it turned out to be true, he would be ready for it; and if it was untrue, he would neither know nor care. Pascal was prudent, if cynical.

In a nutshell, my own position is this: I do not care for the word 'believe' because it sounds too dogmatic, too provable, and we are not talking about things that can be proved; but I trust in the survival of personality after bodily death. As a Christian, I do not think we know much about that condition, or that we could understand it if we were told. And because neither the gospels nor anyone else tell us much about it, I do not actually think we are meant to pay it much attention.

Jesus was urgently concerned with the coming of the kingdom upon earth, which most of his early followers thought would be in their own lifetime. Jesus left no doubt that we would all be subjected to a judgement, as a result of which some would be saved and others destroyed. But the key question upon which judgement would turn was not 'Did you believe the right doctrines, perform the right rituals, observe the letter of the law, guess right about heaven?' The key question would be 'Did you feed the hungry, shelter the homeless, clothe the naked, visit the oppressed?' And that turns our attention firmly to the here and now, towards our living brother and sisters, and away from speculation about harps and roses.

I once asked one of the few really holy bishops I know what he thought death would be like. He answered 'I expect something much bigger than I can imagine, and this frightens me'. And he went on: 'At the moment when time comes to an end for me, I expect to be confronted with the whole of reality in one impact, streaming towards me. At that moment I am either suddenly going to find it in myself to spread my arms, say Yes and jump into the stream; or else I am going to shrink back and say No. I think all the little decisions I am making here in this short life are the decisions as to whether I will ultimately say Yes to reality or whether I will shut myself up in fear and say No, either preparing me for that big Yes or turning me into the kind of person who will finally shrink into nothing.'

In other words, ultimately we judge ourselves, we can choose. In a way we can see this happening in Matthew 25, where the King in judgement sets the sheep on his right hand and the goats on his left and confronts them with their record; for the goats get their chance to repent, to recognize their failure, and do not take it. To the end, they refuse to see God in their fellow men; they decline to accept reality.

Now my first holy bishop was John Vernon Taylor, then of Winchester. In that same series of interviews I talked to an equally holy man, formerly Archbishop Michael Ramsey, and being more of a Catholic than Taylor, he had a different time scale. For you see, one of the details (which I do not personally think is terribly important) is whether we are judged instantly or whether we have to wait for the great universal day of judgement, and whether we wait in dreamless sleep, or in some sort of purgatory trying to improve ourselves. Michael Ramsey is a purgatory man: 'I expect it will be painful', he told me, 'but I know I need a great deal of cleaning up. I do not suppose that just because I die I'm going to get the beatific vision all at once. And it's a pity to leave out hell, because we do need to warn ourselves of it. And I believe in hell [says Ramsey] in this sense: that our free will is a condition of our being moral people; and if our free will were to go on preferring selfish isolation to being joined with the love of God, our free will is quite capable of doing so – and that is hell. I believe hell to be stewing in our own juice, rather than sharing in the love of God. I think we ought to warn ourselves about that, rather than lecturing other people.'

Actually these two good men had a good deal in common, even if John Taylor's purgatory was here and now rather than still to come. You may think that Michael Ramsey's purgatory is a load of Catholic superstition unwarranted in Scripture. But then, as I say, Scripture tells us very little and Ramsey's process has a certain mercy about it, even a certain reasonableness; while his hell of selfishness is really the same as Taylor's No. What neither of them was prepared to do – because neither could presume to imagine it – was to describe heaven in physical terms. It is the consummation of the love of God for the individual human soul: the union or reunion of the two, which is not so far from the Oriental view, except that the Orientals would not retain (and would not wish to retain) our individuality.

I think an important clue lies in John Taylor's remark 'At the moment when time comes to an end for me . . .'. We seem to agree that when we die we no longer have any use for space: heaven and hell have no 'where' no map references or dimensions. But we still seem to think we shall need time: we assume that we may have to spend so many years in purgatory or unconsciousness, or wait so many years to see our loved ones again. When we get to heaven we assume we shall meet those who have got there before us, in time.

But is not all this rather crude? If life after death is beyond space, must it not also be beyond time? I have certain sympathy with a sceptical friend of mine who said he dreaded the idea of eternal life; it sounded like tea at the Savoy for ever, and very, very boring.

And so it would be, unless either we had a further pilgrimage to undertake (perhaps even lives everlasting, one after another) or time vanished and turned out to be the fraud I rather suspect. Could it be that one split second contained everything, past, present and future, and our inability to grasp this is one of the limitations of the human state?

So far I have not stepped much outside the boundaries of traditional Christian mythology; not least, because over the centuries it has proved to be rich and wise and capable of handling most of the higher thoughts we are able to think. But there must be some people present who are eager to press the contributions of spiritualism, of reincarnation, of so-called 'near-death experiences' and those Oriental philosophies seeking to escape the cycle of birth and re-birth.

Of the latter I am afraid I have little to say. You may call it cultural conditioning if you like, but I simply do not think or feel that way, and it would be preposterous for me to pretend to speak for it. The Christian tradition in which most of us were brought up, and which I have learned from experience and example to trust, asserts the value to God of the individual. It sees this life as the process of making a soul – but for what? If there be an afterlife, it would be nonsense for that soul simply to be melted down and returned to the crucible. There is no logical or demonstrable reason why such a melt-down might not happen; but it does not make sense to me as the policy of the God whom I have learned to trust. All this effort, all this glory, and just as you are beginning dimly to understand something: *fizz*. I do not think so.

Spiritualists would say that they know it is not so, because they have made contact with the departed who have told them it is not so. And yet I am afraid I cannot accept the validity of spiritualism, either. It certainly is not scriptural: whatever the risen Christ was, he was not a ghost; nor did he exhort his disciples to commune with the dead. The historic Churches have never accepted such practices, regarding them as (if anything) works of the devil and matters for the exorcist. I would not wish to deprive anyone of the assurance that their loved ones had survived death, but I am bound to say that I am not much impressed by the sheer banality of most messages from beyond the grave seeking to prove it. Frankly, they do not seem worth having. And it would seem to me, in any case, rather bad manners to pester those who must have more important things to do.

There has been a lot of interest recently in the publication of experiences of dying: people who found themselves looking down on their own bodies on the operating table, or felt themselves in a situation remarkably like John Taylor's – rushing towards a great light, only to be called back at the last minute. Mostly these experiences are reported as painless and serene, though there have been a few alarming ones as well.

I have little doubt that these descriptions are perfectly valid; but I also have little doubt that they can be explained in physiological terms or in terms of the electricity of the brain. Dying probably is like that, and it does not sound so bad; but by definition, these are not descriptions of being dead. The truly dead are beyond revival and they certainly do not publish essays about it.

If we are honest with ourselves, I think that we will have to admit that our fascination with life after death has more to do with our fear of dying than with our hope of living on. If there is to be a collapse or concertina-ing of time at the end, it seems possible that there is not going to be much difference between the two: that there might be an intense experience which passes beyond time to become eternal. In which case, since life and death are so closely linked, it might be as well if we took the centuries-old advice of the Church and paid some attention to the readiness of our soul and its attitude to death: to the importance of making peace with one's life in order to have the right perspective on death. When the moment comes, I am sure that one of the key factors will be letting go, as doctors have confirmed to me. Unless both the dying and the surviving are prepared to let go of this life, how can there be another? *Do* go gently into that good night: it was the living poet, not his dying father, who raged against the dying of the light; and clearly it is easier to let go if we trust in the loving God whom we are approaching.

Some of you may be feeling: I do not mind dying myself so much; it is my partner, my child, my friend that I cannot bear to see go. And why does God allow the innocent to die? Surely we deserve something better? But, as another poet once said to me, after losing his wife in tragic circumstances: 'We deserve nothing. For the huge majority of us, it is a privilege to have been here at all, and we have no right to expect to be here tomorrow. Why are we always demanding something better?'

When we think about it, death is actually the inescapable price of life – we cannot have life without it – sooner or later we have to make way for others. It is a mercy that most of us cannot choose or foretell the manner and moment of our dying, that this will be taken care of for us. In the end, the question 'Why me?' gets the answer 'Why *not* you?' It should be perfectly clear to any believer that God does not dish out long life as a reward to the virtuous, or short life as a punishment for the wicked. It does not work like that, and we have the life and death of Jesus to show us this, if nothing else.

It demonstrates also that we have a less good case than we claim for reproaching God with the death of the innocent. In more cases than we care to admit, it is we who are to blame. Floods, famines and earthquakes take some wrestling with (though they are not all that high in the list of the causes of death), but we can hardly blame God for war, terrorism, airline crashes and road casualties. To expect God to go bounding about the universe snatching people from man-made disaster is to regard him as some kind of cosmic nanny, not the loving, anxious, suffering parent of a free people who demand the right to make mistakes.

God has made it open to us to cure one another's diseases if we will to; though even this has become a mixed blessing which prompts the question 'Doctor, what are you going to *let* me die of?' None the less, it is up to us whether we live healthily or poisonously, and whether we produce more children than we can support. For all that I have said about the haphazardness of death, it is less beyond our control than ever before, and so perhaps we have less ground for complaint.

There is no point in bearing a grudge about death. We have the only possible universe that could have produced our kind; and despite the fantasies of science fiction, it still looks like being the only one that did. Somehow it looks increasingly as if the universe was made for us, so it is somewhat impertinent to grumble about the rules. In my experience, people who accept this and are prepared for death are thus admirably prepared for life, and live beautifully.

And yet, and yet . . . I am aware that although it is not exactly easy for me to speak like this, it is an interpretation which not everyone will share. You may say that I have a privileged and successful life, and that I do not know what it is to suffer the extremities of mortal pain or bereavement – both of which are true. I have lain in the Coronary Care Unit, watching my heartbeat blip uncertainly across the monitor screen, experienced the merciful way the body shuts itself down, bit by bit; and I have survived to know that there is nothing to make one grateful for life like a brush with death. Nevertheless, I admit that I am one of the lucky ones. 'Cheer up, we have all got to die, so put your money on Pascal's Best Bet' is not really an adequate pastoral theology. There still remains the bleak question 'Are we just here to die, then? What sort of creator behaves like that?'

A Christian answer might run something like this:

God is love. But the lover needs a beloved. So God made us for himself to love. This is not selfishness on his part, since love is not worth having unless it is freely given, and that freedom gives us the power to reject God's love, Giving us that power is a huge and unselfish sacrifice on God's part. Once we recognize God's love and return it, then only is love circulated and complete, Unrecognized and un-responded-to, it is love crippled and frustrated. And you may say (as I would) that the extreme course of love is to be seen in the love of the parent who gives birth to the child, brings it to maturity and independence, and nurses it even through death. Such a parent is this God I trust in.

But is it *through* death or only *to* death? Well, I have already argued that if there is a God (which I think much more probable than not, although theologically it is not to be proved, or else there would be no atheists) it seems to me absurd that he would have brought us thus far for nothing. But might he not have brought us through simply in order to recycle us, to put us back into the system through some form of reincarnation?

There were certainly notions of this in the minds of those who thought Jesus might have been Elisha, and John the Baptist Elijah. But again, it has no Christian currency; by which I mean that the saints and doctors and Scriptures of the Church will have none of it, nor can I find evidence on which to defy them. If the individual soul really is dear to God for what it is, warts and all, I cannot see why God should want to rub it all out and reissue it as something else. The loving parent does not swap its child for another one, better or worse.

But finally, if you want to know my deepest reason for trusting that death is not the end, it is because (if there is a God) God cannot have an end, God cannot die, and to use the old saying of the Quakers, 'There is that of God in every one'. We all contain the divine spark, the divine image, in a spiritual sense the divine gene. And though on this earth we often ignore it and allow it to become overgrown, it can never be destroyed.

The idea that God is part of us may sound like heresy to some, but it is what the incarnation is all about – God being in humankind. That we are in Christ and Christ in us is deeply scriptural, and all the great mystics have affirmed it.

I think it may even be connected with the mystery of the appearances of the risen Christ. Why did Mary think he was the gardener? Why did the disciples not recognize him on the road to Emmaus, or by the lake shore? I suggest it was because they did not at first realize that he was now in Everyman – that God's immortality is to be in us, just as it will be our immortality to be in him. And I venture to say that just as his survival was made clear through intangible personality – in the end, the disciples could not doubt that it was Jesus, even though his body was changed – so God will know and affirm our personalities when they have left their bodies; our true selves are aspects of him.

Well, we have swum in very deep water – perhaps out of our depth. I do not know whether I have persuaded anyone, depressed anyone, comforted anyone. I can only say that the ordeal has increased my own confidence in our survival, though it is a principle of mine never to claim absolute certainty in anything theological. How could I, when the evidence – what God may see fit to have me experience – is not yet fully laid out, and may never be? In the end, I shall have to decide whether my trust is strong enough to take that leap into the stream, crying Yes. I certainly hope so. And that hope is enormously fortified (as is so much of what passes for my faith) by the examples of other people, people far more spiritually advanced than I, whom I trust and whose lives and personalities persuade me that it is good to do so. I would rather be classed as a fool with them, than sit on the fence being clever.

Perhaps my condition has been best put by John Bunyan in *Pilgrim's Progress*. No, I am not going to read you that triumphant passage where all the trumpets sound on the other side; but the moment when a much humbler character receives his summons:

> Mr Ready-to-Halt called for his fellow pilgrims and told them, saying 'I am sent for, and God shall surely visit you also.' So he desired Mr Valiant to make his will. And because he had nothing to bequeath them that should survive him but his crutches and his good wishes, therefore he said 'These crutches I bequeath to my son that shall tread in my steps, with an hundred warm wishes that he may prove better than I have been.' Then he thanked Mr Great-Heart for his conduct and kindness, and so addressed himself to his journey. When he came to the bank of the river, he said 'Now I shall have no more need of these crutches, since yonder are chariots and horses for me to ride on.' The last words he was heard to say were 'Welcome Life!'
>
> So he went his way.

The author delivered this talk at St Margaret's parish church, Uxbridge, on 24 May 1989, less than a month before suffering his first disabling stroke – as described in the talk which follows. In a memorandum prepared at about the same time, he directed that the passage from *Pilgrim's Progress* quoted above should be read at his own funeral.

18

At a stroke . . .

It is more than a year since I was at the microphone, and even now I am a little uneasy about it. You see, not long ago I had this stroke which left me babbling complete nonsense; and though I think we have got over that, we may need to stop and start the tape while I gather my breath. It is rather an adventure, getting back on the air.

It all started on 22 June last year. The day before, I had driven all the way from Land's End to London, some 350 miles, which I suppose is fairly stressful, but actually I felt quite well as I got up, shaved, and then walked back into the bedroom and began to put my shirt on.

And then I found I could not do the buttons up. Actually, I could not do anything. I sat down on the bed and said to my wife (who was still snoozing in it), 'There's something rather odd about me. Things just aren't working.'

Now my wife normally takes quite a bit of waking up, but this time she immediately snapped into action and telephoned the doctor, who was about to leave for the surgery and diverted himself instead to our house. He was there within ten minutes, and ten minutes after that he was calling the ambulance with the advice that he had a developing case of stroke. The ambulance came promptly and found me woozily insisting that I could walk down the garden path – but I couldn't. I lay in the ambulance watching the coloured light from the wild flowers on Hampstead Heath go by. And then the arrival at the hospital. And then – nothing for a week or two. I am told I was flat out, talking nonsense, while they did various tests on my brain and warned my wife that I would probably never work or walk upstairs again. (I may say that walking upstairs – fairly slowly, admittedly – is one of my specialities today.)

There then passed a very unpleasant week or two – or it

might have been three, or a month – time just did not come into it. In my more lucid moments I just felt sorry for myself – I remember scrawling on a piece of paper the maudlin inscription THE PARTY'S OVER (meaning that I expected to be a permanent invalid), but worst of all were my night fantasies. I imagined I was in an open sarcophagus or tomb, and a procession of mocking figures filed past, silently deriding me. At first they wore costumes of the Italian Renaissance, but later they wore modern dress and were, in fact, figures in the daily life of the hospital; but I believed they were actors who had hired me as a prop in some ghastly play they were rehearsing. The whole thing was enacted in complete silence.

Worst of all, I had lost control of my bowels and my bladder, and much of the time (despite the constant efforts of the staff) I lay stewing in my own filth – my own filth and my own shame, for there is nothing more humiliating to a modestly well-known 62-year-old educated middle-aged man than to be back at the age of two, unable to keep himself clean and wholesome. I wept – it was the blackest depth of my disgrace – until (bless her!) a young nurse put arms round my neck and said 'Gerald, it doesn't matter – it doesn't matter in the least . . .'

And there it was: the beginning of the cure, the redemption, the realization of forgiveness. Sorry to get theological, but for me it was the moment when I realized that love was given and returned regardless of merit, and that when the circle of love is completed like that, nothing can break it. From then on, I got better; the nightmare lifted; my bodily functions pulled themselves together.

I lay in that hospital for more than four months, visited every day by my wife, who became practically a full-time health visitor because our elder daughter (who is now in her thirties) happened to be in the same hospital being treated for cancer. Thank heaven someone in the family was in reasonable health.

It was a good hospital – a credit to Britain's much-criticized health service – modern, light, airy, with fine views over London and pretty good food. Its only faults were a desperate shortage of bedding and nursing staff (both blamed on government economy drives) and an epidemic tendency to lose one's medical records. This was particularly confusing, since the short-term solution was to start another set of records – whereupon the original set would re-emerge and one would be pursued round the hospital by two or three personalities . . .

As for the patients, I soon became aware that our behaviour divided us into two quite distinct categories. Middle-class patients and their visitors are careful to observe the rules, keeping visits short, not more than two visitors to a bed and no small children. A few grapes, one bottle of lemonade and some flowers and books make up the sum of their bedside furnishings. Conversations are kept low and to the point, visits relevant and no more than needed.

The working-class patients have no books and few flowers; but they have up to six bottles of lemonade and a regular bedside fruitstall, including pineapples, melons and a cornucopia of tropical titbits. His or her visitors dress up as if going to church, stay at the bedside for hours and pay no attention to the limitation of numbers; I counted eleven at one bed, including two babies and two squawling toddlers. The patient is propped up on numerous pillows, like the corpse at a Russian funeral, and esteem is shown by the length of the visit. Very little is said by the male visitors, chat being limited almost entirely to the females. The essence of such a visit is generosity, while that of the middle-class visit is economy. It is not done for either group to confess to discomfort or pain. The only exception to this is in patients of Asian origin, where the stiff upper lip is considered out of place and some expression of suffering is regarded as being in good taste.

Most of my fellow patients were of relatively short stay – a week or so, and apparently none the worse off for that – whereas, in the old days, hospital used to be nothing unless you were there for a month at least. The elders of the ward were a group of Scottish and Irish alcoholics who really ought to have been somewhere else – a permanent home or a hostel run by nuns – but it is unfashionable at present to admit this. The fiction is that everyone should be cared for 'in the community', which means that the hopeless cases end up on the streets – so such characters are often to be found failing to fit into the hospitals and even prisons of the land.

On the average they last about two weeks in the reluctant community before they find their way back to the hospital. The Scottish alcoholics in particular seem to have the system mastered. Somehow they manage to get Guinness Stout on prescription every evening, after which they go out drinking in the pub which is (in this case) conveniently situated across the road from the hospital, the bar-room full, half of patients and half of porters, cooks and cleaners. You might have thought the patients would be stopped from making these excursions, but it is part of the philosophy that patients must not be restrained against their will. One evening one of the drinkers from my ward rolled home from the pub, passed out, and was dead by morning. At least he was happier than an epic Irishman who had no legs and existed on a system of tubes and bags. His friends still managed to smuggle him drink, and he was passed round the hospital from ward to ward, roaring that the nurses were out to lay lecherous hands upon his body.

My only escape from this uproar was the daily visit to the Physiotherapy Department, where the girls tried, with some success, to restore movement to my paralysed limbs. Eventually I was sent on to a so-called Rehabilitation Centre, a fairly brutal place, where they took my wheelchair away from me and forced me to do things like walk up stairs and stomp over rough ground. As a result, today I can travel about 200 yards in ten minutes without a walking-stick and I can go up a flight of stairs, though coming down again is a bit scary and everything takes an enormous amount of effort; manoeuvres like going round a corner are full of peril.

I will say this about strokes: you can make progress for the better, unlike things like multiple sclerosis, where you can only get worse. A year ago I was a mumbling pumpkin; now I can type with my left hand and do quite a nice line in left-handed baking, including Dundee cakes and pizzas – though, mind you, it takes all morning. My mental concentration tends to go to pieces after an hour and a half, which is why it has taken five days to write this piece, which I would have tossed off in a morning a year ago.

I am profoundly grateful for what I can do, none the less. By the age of sixty-two I had had at least two good lives, one as a foreign correspondent and one as an author, and burnt the candle at every conceivable end: anything more is supererogatory grace. My chief complaints are simple, physical ones: it hurts. My right side feels as if it had been rolled in a bed of nettles, and my right foot feels as if it had been jammed in a mincing machine. My right hand does not feel anything. But this is so perpetual that it is boring. The question that so many people suppose must be bothering me, does not bother me at all – namely, 'Why me? Why has life been so unfair to me?' Well – why ever *not* me?

We have the only possible universe that could have produced us, and part of the price of this incredible bargain is that we all have to die of something and one in two hundred of us gets a stroke. Sooner that than cancer of the lower bowel: I am the ideal person to get a stroke, because I have done most of the things I wanted to do, and I am quite content to sit the rest of the rat race out. I can amuse myself now with little triumphs like getting a new ribbon into my typewriter, or having a sly letter printed in *The Times*: triumphs that keep me happy for days, and signal to the world from time to time that I am still here, on the sidelines of life, maybe, but still punctuating the game with the occasional comment.

In fact, thanks to my friends, I can do more than that. This is where old friends really come into their own, for it is wonderful what you can do in Britain as a disabled person with somebody to telephone ahead, push your chair, drive the car: you can do almost anything any normal person can do if only you have a bit of help. You want to go to the Art Gallery, and provided somebody warns them that you are coming, then parking places are reserved in the choicest places, lifts are revealed in unlikely corners, and you are wafted into the heart of the Royal Academy, the Tate Gallery or the grand new Courtauld Institute, way ahead of the mob.

And when it comes to opera, of which I am a particular devotee, then I would almost recommend becoming a cripple: you present yourself at the doors of the Royal Opera House, a dozen stout hands seize your wheelchair, and in a trice you are manhandled into the best seats in the house at a price which is derisory – a mere fraction of what everyone else is paying. The same is true of the national theatres: nothing is too good for us poor cripples; and there is even a car which will take me and my chair there and back, subsidized by the local authority.

I will not say that the benefits paid me by the Government are enough to live on, but they are a very considerable help. I can actually keep on living in the house that I had before, without having to move somewhere cheaper and nastier. Oh, we have to economize, and sometimes our financial arithmetic is so precarious one can only laugh at it: last month we ended up nine pounds this side of disaster: but – and I cannot think of any other word – we are *happy*. Today's special is the white lily – *lilium regale* – at the end of my garden, flooding the place with an intoxicating but frankly rather common fragrance. Happily I bask in its cheap luxury. The Grim Reaper has taken a first swipe at me – *and missed*.

This talk was broadcast as a 'Personal View' on the BBC World Service, in September 1990.

19
A nasty way to die

Christ is risen! Death is conquered! The grave is empty! This is the whole point of the Christian faith in which I – as an old-fashioned liberal Christian after the school of the Bishop of Durham – wholeheartedly believe. But I believe it because I believe most thoroughly that Christ was dead: I believe in the crucifixion as a fact and not as a tableau in an altar-piece. I believe that he was crucified, dead and buried; and that we do not give enough thought to this. Knowing the triumph that is to come, we hurry on and do not care to give one Saturday's contemplation to the moment of the *failure* of Christianity, and hence to the full range of its achievement as a success. Jesus died – and it was a very nasty way to die indeed.

As a journalist for more than forty years, I have had my fill of executions. I have seen a prime minister hanged, very slowly, from a low tripod. I have seen a sodomite gassed. I have seen a row of black marketeers shot – and I will spare you the details, which are always messy. The worst thing, perhaps, is the way authority tries to look stately on these occasions and ends up looking ridiculous and embarrassed – all so different from the impartial punishment which the advocates of capital punishment imagine. The only exception is the old-fashioned blood bath, the public execution where we are all animals together and a roar goes up as the axe flashes and the head is held high with closed eyes and lips parted – that is the real spirit of execution. Unless you have been there and felt yourself part of the lynch-mob, it is a mere anecdote at second-hand.

This has always seemed to me the essence of the reporter's task: to convey what it is like to be there. Too many journalists nowadays sound as if they were writing their accounts from the news agency tape. In any case we have to rely on sources even more remote for our accounts of the crucifixion, though they are remarkably full and varied for so distant an event. They have been overlaid with an atmosphere of formality and ceremony which takes us out of the realm of journalism and into the worlds of art and symbolism and theology. Because we know what comes next we find it almost impossible to concentrate on what the act of crucifixion itself was really like. But to everyone involved at the time it was the end of the story, the one reality. Nor was it in the least like a church crucifixion, a Renaissance painting tidied up, with angels catching a few drops of blood in goblets, and a discreet loincloth to hide the nakedness of an almost weightless Christ (the spectators about to return their costumes to the wardrobe mistress before going home) – it was not like that at all.

Perhaps the main point to be grasped about the death of Jesus is that it was not only extremely painful and protracted, but was deliberately meant to be utterly final. It was a form of execution reserved by the Romans almost exclusively for the terrorization of the slave population and the deterrence of treason, and it was particularly dreadful in Jewish eyes – dreadful, shameful and disgusting. You will recall how St Paul says: 'We proclaim Christ crucified, even though this is a stumbling block to the Jews . . . We make light of its disgrace . . . Christ bought us freedom from the curse of the law by becoming (for our sake) an accursed thing; for Scripture says a curse is on everyone who is hanged on a gibbet.'

At this point St Paul is quoting from the ancient Jewish law as found in Deuteronomy 21. 22–23:

> 'And if a man have committed a sin worthy of
> death and he be put to death and thou hang him
> on a tree: His body shall not remain all night upon
> the tree, but thou shalt in any wise bury him that
> day; (for he that is hanged is accursed of God;) that
> thy land be not defiled, which the Lord thy God
> giveth thee for an inheritance.'

The reference here is to the exhibition of a dead body, not to a lingering execution; but the point, as Paul makes perfectly clear, is that the gibbet is defiling, and it is worth noting that the ritual described by the gospels shows a nice awareness of the necessary details of burial.

Again, if you look in the Vatican collection of early Christian sculpture (including numerous items from the catacombs) you will hardly find a single representation of the crucified Christ. Until about the fifth century the iconography steers clear of it and prefers the Good Shepherd or the True Vine – anything but the figure of agony and humiliation. Like hanging, drawing and quartering within our own reach, such a figure was hardly the subject for art.

This is hardly surprising, for within fifty years of the death of Jesus, crucifixion had been given an extra layer of horror. Let me quote from the historian Josephus, in his description of the siege of Jerusalem in AD 70:

> Jewish prisoners were first whipped and then tormented with all sort of tortures and were then crucified before the walls of the city. Titus (the Roman conqueror) felt pity for them, but as their number – up to five hundred a day – was too great for him to risk either letting them go or putting them under guard, he allowed his soldiers to have their way, especially as he hoped the gruesome sight of the countless crosses might move the besieged to surrender. So the soldiers, out of the rage and hatred they bore the prisoners, nailed those they caught in different postures to the crosses, by way of amusement. And their number was so great that there was not enough room for the crosses, and not enough crosses for the bodies.

This was only one of many exhibitions of this kind mounted by Roman armies in the ancient world; a kind of official terrorism at which the aristocracy shuddered, but insisted that it was the only language that the lower orders understood. Thus we find the great classical barrister, Cicero, speaking in the first century BC, saying 'The very name of the cross should never come near the person of a Roman citizen, nor even enter his thoughts, his sight or his hearing'. Elsewhere Cicero describes the cross as 'that scourge . . . the most repulsive and horrible form of death'. A Roman citizen was supposed to be exempt from crucifixion; hence you find most of the early writers referring to Christians as mad or depraved for worshipping an alleged god who had suffered the death reserved for the lowest form of criminals. 'Folly to the Greeks' says St Paul, for it was obvious to the Greeks that the gods were immortal: it was sheer foolishness to try and sell them a god who (even if he had risen again from the tomb) had allowed himself such undignified exposure. A half-hearted way round this – which, incidentally, you will find in the Koran – is what is known as Docetism, the doctrine that Jesus did not really die on the cross at all, that it was only an appearance, a shadow of him that died there, and maybe even a substitute: the real Jesus was carried straight to heaven. It was to stamp out this kind of rumour from the start that St John's gospel makes all that fuss about St Thomas demanding to touch the wounds of the risen Christ.

What Paul is saying, then, is that whether you are trying to sell the good news of Jesus to the Jews or to the Greeks, you have a pretty unsaleable item on your hands. A god who is accursed and unclean – and a god who is actually *dead*? Paul and the early Christians were trying to market a revolutionary, upside-down sort of god. Instead of a supreme king in glory he had first to be accepted as the lowest kind of slave, butchered like an animal. Christians today tend to assume that we can easily take this as read. But I am suggesting that it presented a problem which was insuperable, and the fact that it was overcome, in those first two or three centuries of faith, is something that we must accept even if we cannot entirely understand it.

So far we have concentrated on the political – shall I say law and order? – aspect of the crucifixion. I ought to say something about the physical side of it, because it is the personal side, the side that really *is* incarnational, God made all too intimately flesh.

Crucifixion was only the climax of a way of death. First came the torture, the scourging and mocking, and the forced carrying of one's own heavy cross (or maybe the cross-piece), for which Jesus was evidently too weak to complete the course. Then the nailing to the cross. We know now how it was done, which was not the way it usually appears in paintings. That mysterious relic, the Holy Shroud of Turin, though a pious fraud (I am afraid), has got it right: two nails went through the wrists – not the hands – because nails through the palms of the hands would not have supported the weight of the body.

A Frenchman called Barbet demonstrated this by some rather gruesome experiments in the 1930s. In the same way, two other experimenters found that if you simply suspended the body from the wrists, with an additional nail through the ankles, it was then extremely difficult to breathe in and out, so that the victim (in this case the experimenters themselves, using rope lashings rather than nails) began to lose consciousness after twelve to twenty minutes, which was not at all the drawn-out agony which the Roman executioner sought. The Romans were not normally interested in as quick a death as that Christ underwent: they commonly provided an additional means of support, either a kind of foot rest or a small wooden seat (no more than a peg, really) upon which the victim squirmed in search of a rest that was no rest.

We still cannot say exactly how Jesus of Nazareth was crucified, because there really was no standard form. Some crosses had the familiar Christian shape, others were T-shaped, others again diagonal (the so-called St Andrew's cross) and on some we know the victims were hung upside down. The chances are that Jesus received a fairly orthodox execution, for we are told that his two fellow-victims (who presumably had been able to sit back and avoid suffocating themselves) had to have their legs broken so as to force their weight onto their arms, and thus hasten death before sunset; whereas Jesus, already weak from loss of blood, was unable to keep himself on the wooden peg and was dead. The spear in the side proved that; and if there was one thing the execution squad could have been relied upon to certify, it was that its victims were dead.

I have read half a dozen books arguing that in some way Jesus was *not* dead, that the haste of the occasion enabled his followers to revive him. But there are many reasons why that will not stand up, chief among them that it is not what the four gospels allow, and the gospels are incomparably older than any other source. They are confused, they are not sure what did happen, but their very lack of neatness is convincing. Above all, Paul – whose job it was, originally, to expose the Christian racket, and who must have heard and investigated all the stories about it – was more convinced than anyone of its truth. It is not my present concern to write the next chapter of this story, which is just as well, for I do not pretend to know exactly what happened. But that something extraordinary happened, which compelled the belief of the early Christians against all probability, that I must believe.

I believe it all the more because of the unpleasant, fleshly facts which I have recounted. One reason why – which I mention with some reluctance, because in comparison with the suffering of Jesus it is trivial – is that I am in constant pain myself. Nobody is maliciously torturing me, it is just one of the pains that flesh is heir to. I have been fitted with a little electric box which is supposed to deaden it (not, I am afraid, very successfully). It is in no way comparable with being crucified; but it is a reminder that pain can be the one reality in one's life, it can be the only thing that anyone – even the Son of God – is able to think about. It is, perhaps the ultimate. Is it hell?

I do not know. But I do know that at the end, as one gets near the edge, the body has a merciful way of 'switching off' the sensations that it cannot stand, of narrowing down its sensations to the essential. I have had the feeling of being crushed under a rock till I could see only one crack of light, and that was the love of God, the absolute certainty, when everything else had been taken from me, that God loved me. And then, of course, things widened again and all sorts of bodily inconveniences came back, one by one – you cannot call it the sensation of having died. But it has been a comfort to me ever since, and I have liked to think that round the corner of his supreme agony there lay waiting for Jesus that same assurance that in the end and in spite of it all, his Father loved him, and all manner of thing would be well.

For this 1991 Lent Talk, given on BBC Radio 4, the author took an earlier, undated script on the same theme and re-worked the conclusion in terms of his own recent experience.

20

Striking out, after a stroke

(*In medical terms the writer suffered a cerebro-vascular accident on 22 June 1989 which resulted in dysphasia and right-side hemiparesis.*)

We are just coming up to the second anniversary of my stroke, which we shall be celebrating with some quite creditable New Zealand champagne, for I have a lot to be thankful for.

The chief thing you need to survive a stroke is a good stroke-resistant wife. But you have to contrive that, as far as possible, she manages to carry on with her own life, doing her own things as well as most of yours; and this means the stricken has to resist the temptation to become a victim, a full-time sufferer. So I dress myself, though it takes an hour, and wash up the breakfast things. My right leg hurts like hell, in spite of various interesting experiments by the medical profession. But since the reader cannot share it with me I will put that grumble away for the duration. I have as rich and enjoyable a life as any 64-year-old I know.

After four months in hospital and twenty months at home again, I suppose I have reached the plateau of my recovery. My right arm is fairly useless and my walking is limited. My range, unaided, is no more than a hundred yards very slowly; though we can extend it, of course, with the NHS wheelchair and the car (which my wife has to drive). I can get around the house and into the garden, but uneven surfaces and slopes alarm me. I suppose I get out about three times a week, including a modest weekly visit to the wine merchant which gives me great pleasure.

Some of the local Hampstead pubs – notably the Old Bull and Bush – have convenient parking and see me for the odd pint, but the truth is I was never very clubbable and prefer the solitude of my study, looking down a green garden, to any bar or dining room.

Hampstead suits me very well, for Kenwood, Golders Hill Park and Regent's Park are ideal wheelchair country. My wife's pushing-power is limited to gentle gradients, and if I want to tackle anything more ambitious I have to summon one of a handful of sturdy friends. With George at the handlebars, for example, I have cruised Brent Cross Shopping Centre (which is cripple-friendly) and gone as far as Amersham after pheasants for the freezer, or Berkhamsted for trout.

But my most ambitious outings are a night at the opera, Covent Garden, no less, though let me add that I recently had a stirring night out at the ENO's *Peter Grimes*.

It is the Royal Opera House, though, that treats us poor unfortunates so royally, tearing out what I reckon to be the second best seats in the house to make room for our wheelchairs and plying us with sandwiches and ice-cream in the intervals. On special evenings they have a kind of wheelchair rally with up to fourteen of the hideous things lined up along the front row of the tier.

The process of getting us there is even more spectacular. We line up along the pavement outside in Floral Street and gangs of volunteers hurl us up through the staircases into the auditorium like shells being loaded into a battleship. All thanks to the benefactor who makes it possible for us to be there, and to be there at a cost – only fifteen pounds plus the same for our minder – which is barely a fifth of what anyone else has to pay. If you are an opera fan as I am, it is almost worth getting disabled. I can now go about once a month, just as I had (for financial reasons) regretfully decided that I would have to give up the Garden forever.

I am not such a fan of the theatre, but I know from experience that the National is equally generous. And the National Art Collections do their best within their quaint limits. The Tate uses a huge sculpture elevator. The Courtauld has a curious lift in a cupboard, and another on the way out which looks like a method of execution. My curses, by the way, on all those able-bodied motorists who park on our reserved parking-places.

On the whole I do not feel inclined to join any organization of discontented cripples (for that is what we are: not coyly Disabled Persons, which is what officialdom would like us to be). I really am pretty content with what the community does for me.

But no two strokes are quite the same. For myself, I am more concerned with my mental than with my physical condition, which is what you might expect of an elderly man of letters. Everything takes enormous effort. I can just about manage an article like this, though it has taken me three days to peck out with one finger of my hand, where once I could have done it in a morning. But I can hold my own in conversation now, and my vocabulary is 90 per cent what it once was. The other day the word 'profuse' came home to its kennel, wagging its tail. My ability to do mental arithmetic and to tell right from left seem to have been completely destroyed; but my musical bump is unscathed.

So, as I say, I have a lot to be thankful for. I have lost three stone I did not need, and keep them lost by two devices. Thanks, as ever, to my wife, I eat sparingly but choice. And I only drink alcohol on Fridays, Saturdays and Sundays, not Mondays to Thursdays. My major regret is that one-handed men cannot open oysters, which must be the ideal slimmers' food. Meanwhile I am saving up for one of those electrically propelled wheelchairs.

The planned anniversary celebration mentioned in this piece never took place, as the author suffered a second and fatal stroke on the morning of that day.

21
Face to faith

I once promised a friend that I would write an absolutely honest examination of my faith in God; 'Because if you do', he said, 'I don't see how you can do it. Cut out all that wishful thinking and theological gobbledegook, and arguments which you would never allow in any other case, and you can only say "This is something different – other categories of thought and language do not apply". Which is a cop-out.'

My friend inconsiderately then died, so I suppose he may now know the answer better than I do. That is, supposing he knows anything. I have always found a certain dishonest comfort in what is known as Pascal's Best Bet: that is, it is the best bet to believe in God, because if there is a God the believer will have the advantage in heaven; and if there is not, it does not matter because he will not know or care anyway. In one sense, I cannot lose. In another, I may face a fearful punishment.

I am prepared, you see, to put up with a good deal of uncertainty; in fact it is vital to my concept of God. I think we have to be uncertain about God both because it is impossible that we should know more than a fraction of him – because if we thought we understood him we should quite certainly be wrong – and because I think it is in his nature to be uncertain, changing, as elusive as the cuckoo who escaped from the men who sought to enclose the Spring.

So to my friend, I am afraid, I would seem to be cheating from the start. I have to admit – for it is part of my faith – that I may be wrong, that there may not be a God at all. I could not believe in a God who had to exist. He must be voluntary or not exist. A compulsory God, a God in whom we had to believe because it was impossible to believe otherwise, would either be a tyrant or so dreary that there was nothing to discuss about him. (It would be impossible, for example, to write this essay.) In any case we could not act *as if* he did not exist, which we frequently do even if we believe in him.

But all this is juggling with words, or seems to be, because I can make the words go no further along this track. What reasons have I got even for behaving at least some of the time as if there were a God?

In the Victorian age I might have taken my stand on the argument from design, and asserted that the orderliness and majesty of the universe indicated the existence of a Supreme Architect. I might have insisted that the mounting evidence that only this particular finely tuned universe could have produced humankind was a virtual confirmation of Genesis. But I fear that science and its works are unreliable and divided allies for theology, and today's evidence of divine order becomes tomorrow's nihilistic chaos. In the end, what science is concerned with is not really what religion is about.

Today I am much moved by direct religious experience. There have been moments in my life when I have felt the intervention of something greater than, and outside, myself; when guiding words have formed in my head; when, close to death, I have been intensely aware of what I could only call the love of God. But I cannot prove – I cannot be sure – that these experiences are not the unconscious fulfilment of wishes, or the working of my consciousness upon the chemical processes of the brain. Perhaps those moments of vast awareness glimpsed on the cliffs at sunset are really no more than aesthetic experience.

Some readers may blame me for refusing to accept evidence which, they say, is quite enough for the average human being. But it seems to me that the assertion we seek to verify – namely that God exists – is by far and away the greatest, most serious that we can possibly make. Its truth or falsehood ought to make all the difference to how we live (and yet does it? and if it does not, what is the implication of that?).

In the end, I find that the most cogent proof for me of God's existence is what I will call – though Quakers must wince at the title – the argument from the Church: the fact that for two thousand years (and in fact more) people have believed, people ranging from simple peasants to giant intellects.

This, or course, is even more vulnerable as an argument than the others; for 'giant intellects' have believed a great many things which we laugh to scorn today – they have believed in devils, ghosts, witchcraft, and none of us need reminding of the absurdities and cruelties practised by the churches of yesterday and even today.

Yet the Church I mean is something above and beyond this, and it resides very much in its saints (of whom Quakers have had quite as many *pro rata* as any other gathering). But let me try to sum it up in the words of a great philosopher who happened to be a Roman Catholic:

> I have moments when I feel it is a question of hanging on, in the sense of loyalty. It's not that I don't want to let myself down, but the few lives that are devoted to the love of God: not only those who risk martyrdom, but who give up their lives to the relief of suffering or to penance and contemplation. The one thing I feel I cannot do is adopt a view of the world which would make nonsense of such lives. When it comes to it, that is where my loyalty lies.

This talk was in the author's typewriter at his death. He almost certainly intended to revise it further: four paragraphs from the end, the word SCRIPTURE appears in the margin, but is not followed up.

When he came to the bank of the river, he said 'Now I shall have no more need of these crutches, since yonder are chariots and horses for me to ride on.' The last words he was heard to say were 'Welcome Life!'

Pilgrim's Progress